MW01622853

THE BOOK OF THE SAVIOUR

Volume Two: The Proclamation of the Kingdom

THE BOOK OF THE SAVIOUR

VOLUME ONE: THE INCARNATION

VOLUME TWO: THE PROCLAMATION OF THE KINGDOM

VOLUME THREE: THE PASCHAL MYSTERY

THE BOOK OF THE SAVIOUR

Volume Two: The Proclamation of the Kingdom

Assembled by F. J. SHEED

CLUNY
Providence, Rhode Island

CLUNY MEDIA EDITION, 2023

This Cluny edition is a republication, in part, of
The Book of the Saviour (Part II: The Public Ministry Years),
originally published by Sheed & Ward, Inc., in 1952.

For more information regarding this title
or any other Cluny Media publication,
please write to info@clunymedia.com, or to
Cluny Media, P.O. Box 1664, Providence, RI 02901

VISIT US ONLINE AT WWW.CLUNYMEDIA.COM

Cluny Media edition copyright © 2023 Cluny Media LLC

ISBN: 978-1685951795 || *All rights reserved.*

NIHIL OBSTAT: John J. Consodine, *Diocesan Censor*

IMPRIMATUR: Richard J. Cushing, *Archbishop of Boston*
MAY 12, 1952

Cover design by Clarke & Clarke
Cover image: Bartolomé Esteban Murillo,
The Healing of the Paralytic, 1667–1670, oil on canvas
Courtesy of Wikimedia Commons

CONTENTS

What I was born for, what I came into the world for,
is to bear witness of the truth.

(JOHN 18:37)

❧

F. J. SHEED

PROLOGUE

I

From the first man, Adam, we are all sprung; in him the whole human race was incorporated, since there is no one of us that does not come from him; he *was* the whole human race when God made him. Adam had the natural life that made him man—the union of spiritual soul and material body which constituted his nature as man, without which he would not have been man: and this natural life he had in a state of perfection, all his powers and faculties rightly ordered, body subordinate to soul, soul ruled by reason. He also had the Supernatural Life—the life above nature—that whereby he would be able to live the life of Heaven hereafter, whereby even in this life his whole soul was "supernaturalized," capable of a relationship with God altogether higher and holier than anything that could take its rise in man's merely natural endowments. The highest and holiest point of this relationship and the very condition of the Supernatural Life was for Adam, as it is for all men, the union of the soul with God by love. And while he had the Supernatural Life, God also exempted his nature from the law of death—from the separation of soul and body which is the natural termination of man's life on this earth.

For Adam the simplest elements of the road of human life were two, not three—his entry into life was at one end and Heaven was at the other: death did not lie in between. That, simply and directly, was God's scheme. And man wrecked the scheme. Adam sinned, rebelled against God; and thereby lost the Supernatural Life, for this Life cannot exist where the love of God is not, and love of Him cannot exist where there is rebellion against Him. Scripture represents the sinful action as the eating of the fruit of the forbidden tree. There is some mystery here. But two things about it we know. The first is that it was a sin of disobedience to God. The second is that the Devil played a part in it.

It is important to understand Adam's new condition. He had lost the Supernatural Life: he retained the natural life, or the union of body and soul; the soul retained the natural powers of intellect and will. Supernaturally he was dead, for the loss of life is death; naturally he still lived. But even his nature did not emerge from the disaster unimpaired. It lost the privilege of exemption from death; henceforth man must pass through the gateway of death to reach his eternal destiny. More serious still was that man's nature lost its *direction.* Adam had sinned because he had chosen his own will instead of God's—he had swung his nature out of its true Godward direction, and had introduced war into the very inmost part of his nature, into the union of body and spirit—body warring against spirit, spirit torn by war in its own powers.

Thus then stood Adam, the *individual* man—the Supernatural Life lost, the natural life impaired because given a wrong direction; but still knowing the purpose of his being and the laws set by God for the governance of his life. But Adam was also, by God's dispensation, the *representative* man, and the effect of this catastrophe upon the whole human race is measureless. As a mere physical consequence the nature he had to hand on to his descendants was an impaired nature, strongly attracted to sin. Worse than that: in Adam the race lost the Supernatural Life: so that men thereafter (with one glorious exception) were to enter this world with the natural life of soul and body but without the Supernatural Life: the right relationship of oneness between God and the human race was broken and Heaven was closed to man.

The problem for the human race was precisely the restoration of the broken oneness with God: it was the problem of atonement, which we disguise by the pronunciation *atonement.* God knew how He would solve the problem: how the human race might be re-united with Him. And it can hardly be for nothing that the first statement God made of what He would do, He made not to Adam, but to the Devil, and He made it in terms of victory over the Devil: his head was to be crushed.

II

In God's plan for the re-establishment of the whole race, a special part was to be acted by one race, the Jews, and because of this God brought them into a special relation with Himself. This special relation of one people with God begins at a time and a place—the time roughly 2000 B.C., the place Haran in the land of Chanaan. There had come Abram, with his father and his brothers, from the Chaldean town of Ur. And God said to Abram (Gen. 11): "I will make of thee a great nation, and I will bless thee and magnify thy name: and thou shalt be blessed. I will bless them that bless thee and curse them that curse thee; and in thee shall all the kindred of the earth be blessed." In the years that followed, God renewed the promises many times: but it was twenty-five years later that the great covenant was made which constituted the Jews God's people (Gen. 17): "God said to him: I *am*. And my covenant is with thee; and thou shalt be a father of many nations... And I will establish my covenant between me and thee, and between thy seed after thee in their generations, by a perpetual covenant: to be a God to thee, and to thy seed after thee." God changed Abram's name to Abraham, which means "father of nations" and gave the command of circumcision "as a sign of the covenant."

God then had singled out a particular family which was to grow into a nation: not for their own sake but for the sake of all mankind: they were chosen not simply for a favour but for a function, something God was to do through them for the whole race. This God makes clear again (Gen. 22): "In thy seed shall all the nations of the earth be blessed."

These promises were repeated to Abraham's second son Isaac (he had already had a son Ishmael by a bondwoman) and to Isaac's second son Jacob (for the elder, Esau, had foresworn his birthright). In all this we see the hint of Redemption—all mankind is to be blessed through the seed of Abraham. And soon comes the hint of a Redeemer, and even of the mode of the Redemption—Jacob, dying, prophesies one who is to come from his fourth son Judah: "The sceptre shall not be taken away from Judah, nor a ruler from his thigh, till he come that is to be sent: and he shall be the expectation of nations. Tying his foal to the vineyard, and his ass, O my son, to the vine: He shall wash his robe in wine and his garment in the blood of the grape." (Gen. 49:10–11).

By now the children of Jacob, to whom God had given the new name of Israel, were in Egypt, and there they were to be for four hundred years. The last part of that time they were fiercely oppressed, until God brought them out of Egypt under the leader Moses, whom he had appointed to them. The last act of their time in Egypt was spectacular. The angel of God visited the houses of the Egyptians slaying the first-born, but he passed over the houses of the children of Israel, who had marked their door-posts with the blood of a lamb sacrificed by God's ordinance. And God ordered that this passing over (pasch is the Hebrew word) should be celebrated each year by the sacrifice and eating of a lamb.

So the Israelites went from Egypt, crossed the Red Sea and came into the Arabian Desert: and there, upon Mt. Sinai, the Covenant was renewed and the Law was given. God gave the Jews, through Moses, the Ten Commandments and a great mass of moral, ritual and legal precepts covering every detail of their lives. Sacrifices were offered and Moses "taking the book of the covenant" read it in the hearing of all the people: and they said, "All things that the Lord hath spoken, we will do. We will be obedient. And he took the blood and sprinkled it upon the people, and he said: *This is the blood of the covenant* which the Lord has made with you concerning all these words" (Ex. 24).

Let us repeat that the Jews were chosen because of something God meant to accomplish through them for the whole world. The essence of their function lay in this—that from them was to come the Redeemer, who should redeem all mankind. Meanwhile, they were to bear witness to truths which were in danger of perishing, which indeed seemed to have perished utterly: the truth that there is but one God, the truth that God will send a Redeemer of mankind.

Observe that the Jews showed no great natural aptitude for, or any very tenacious hold upon, either truth. Monotheism, for instance, made no more appeal to them than to all that ocean of polytheistic people which surrounded them. All their instincts ran to strange gods and to idols: the thing seems to have been a craving as strong as a man might feel for alcohol. They were forever going after the ways of the heathen, and God forever restoring them to right ways. God's pedagogy was of two sorts: He allowed their enemies to work their will upon them as a reminder that they were in the hand of the one God and could achieve nothing without Him: He sent them the Prophets to bear glowing and glorious witness to the same truth. If the Jews found monotheism difficult, they found not much easier the doctrine as to the nature of the Messiah, the Anointed One, who was to come, and of the Kingdom He was to found. Here again the Prophets were their instructors, and as the centuries pass the picture of the Messiah grows in detail and in clarity.

Yet we should be mistaken if we exaggerated the clarity. There is a vast mass of prophecy and a magnificence over all of it. But much of it is obscure even to us who have seen its fulfilment; certain elements which now seem most wonderfully fulfilled appear buried in their context, not emphasized as prophetical or especially likely to catch the ear or the eye. The Prophets did not provide a blackboard diagram and then proceed to lecture on it. Indeed our modern use of the word prophet may give us a wrong notion of their office. To prophesy does not mean to foretell but to speak out. They were not there primarily to foretell the future but to utter the eternal and judge the present by it. The Jews not unnaturally found morality harder even than monotheism: the Law had imposed on them a morality stricter than any known to men, and they fell from it. The Prophets thundered against this as against strange gods. For here too they must judge the present by the eternal.

But precisely because that was their function they did speak much of Him who was to come. Consider how the picture builds up. We have already seen that One who was to be the expectation of nations should come from Judah. From the Psalms (e.g., Ps. 131:11) we gather the further detail that He was to be a descendant of David the King, and this is confirmed by the statement of Isaiah (11:1) that he is to be "a rod out of the root of Jesse," for Jesse was David's father: "In that day, the root of Jesse, who standeth for an ensign of the people, him the Gentiles shall beseech: and his sepulchre shall be glorious." There is no explicit statement that this is the Messiah: but St. Paul takes it for granted (Rom. 15:12), and in any event no Jew doubted that the Messiah was to be sprung from David.

In the seventh chapter of Isaiah we read "Behold a virgin shall conceive and bear a son: and his name shall be called Emmanuel.' From St. Matthew (1:23) we know that this is a prophecy of the virgin birth of Christ; yet in the context, one might well think that the prophecy referred to an event immediately expected and actually described in the next chapter of Isaiah, the eighth, as having happened. In the light of our new knowledge, we can re-read the eighth chapter and see that though there is some sort of fulfilment there and then, yet some mightier thing is involved: the language used is of a grandeur too great for the actual episode.

The fifth chapter of Micah tells us that the Messiah is to be born in Bethlehem: "And thou, Bethlehem Ephrata, art a little one among the thousands of Judah: out of thee shall he come forth unto me that is to be the ruler in Israel: and his going forth is from the beginning, from the days of eternity.... And this man shall be our peace."

There are other details which we see fulfilled, but which could hardly have meant so much to their first hearers: thus Zachariah (9:9) writes: "Rejoice greatly, O daughter of Sion, shout for joy, O daughter of Jerusalem: Behold thy King will come to thee, the just and saviour. He is poor and riding upon an ass, upon a colt, the foal of an ass."

Such details as we have been considering—that the Messiah was to be of the tribe of Judah, of the family of David, born of a virgin and in Bethlehem—are not the primary things about Him. Two things that matter far more are Himself and what He was to do. Upon both, the prophecies are fuller and clearer.

As to what He was; there is a central stream of teaching which shows Him a man triumphant, and two parallel streams, one showing Him as more than a man, the other showing Him as less than triumphant. It would seem that the Jews concentrated on the central stream, and made little of either of the others. Yet these others are of such vast importance, that missing them one hardly sees Him at all.

That He was to be more than man, not simply the greatest of men, is indicated again and again. We have already seen the phrase of Micah—"his going forth is from the beginning, from the days of eternity." The same truth is to be found in Psalm 109—"before the day star, I begot thee." But it is not only by pre-existence that the Messiah seems to be more than man. The hints are everywhere—as for instance in the suggestion that He is to be son to God in a special way. (It is hard to see how they could be more than hints: the truth about the divinity of the Messiah could not well be conveyed to a nation that did not know the doctrine of the Trinity.)

The reverse of the medal is the even clearer stream of prophecy that the Messiah is to be poor and suffering. The greatest passages are in Psalm 21 and in Chapter 53 of Isaiah. The Psalm and the Chapter should be read most carefully. Here note a few verses from the Chapter, summing all up:

> Despised and the most abject of men, a man of sorrows and acquainted with infirmity....
>
> He shall be led as a sheep to the slaughter and shall be dumb as a lamb before his shearer....
>
> And the Lord was pleased to bruise him in infirmity. If he shall lay down his life for sin, he shall see a long-lived seed....

To say that the Jews ignored a good deal of all this is not to accuse them of any startling malignity. The assertion of the Messiah's pre-existence, for example, was difficult to reconcile with the certainty that he was to be a descendant of David: one gets the impression that the Jews, faced with two elements difficult to reconcile, simply took the intellectual line of least resistance, concentrated upon the clearer one and left the other in its mysteriousness. Similarly it is hard to see how anything short of what did in fact happen to Christ Our Lord could have shown the fulfilment both of the splendour and the suffering: lacking that clue, they concentrated on the more obvious.

But if their intellect followed the line of least resistance in the picture they formed of the Messiah in Himself, their will seems to have followed the line of greatest complacency in the picture they formed of the Kingdom He was to found. They saw it as a Kingdom of Israel in which the Gentiles, if they came into it at all, should be very much in a subordinate place; and they saw it as an earthly and not as a spiritual Kingdom. The Prophets, properly read, supply correctives for both.

Thus they assert that the Messiah is coming for a light to the Gentiles and that the Gentiles are to share in the joy of His Kingdom. When Psalm 71 says: "In him shall all the tribes of the earth be blessed: all nations shall magnify him," it simply reasserts what God said to Abram in the first of the promises. Isaiah is filled with the same teaching: and he indicates the possibility that there may be Jews excluded from the Kingdom and Gentiles admitted. So St. Paul (Rom. 10:20) explains the contrast (Isaiah 65) between what God says of the Gentiles: "Those who never looked for me have found me: I have made myself known to those who never asked for word of me," and what He says of the Jews: "I stretch out my hand all day to a people that refuses obedience and cries out against me." But if we find from the Prophets that the Gentiles were to have a place, and a place of joy in the Kingdom, it was left for St. Paul to utter in plain words the intimate secret of the total equality of Jew and Gentile in the Kingdom, the mystery of Christ "which was never made known to any human being in past ages… that through the gospel preaching the Gentiles are to win the same inheritance, to be made part of the same body, to share the same divine promise in Christ Jesus" (Eph. 3:5–6).

Thus all who belong to Christ are of the seed of Abraham, and the promises of the Kingdom are to us. But what sort of Kingdom? The Jews, as we have seen, seemed to expect an earthly Kingdom. The Prophets do not precisely and explicitly contradict them, but they give a mass of teaching which should have made the notion of a merely earthly Kingdom untenable and not even desirable. Thus Ezekiel (36:24–26): "And I will pour upon you clean water and you shall be cleansed from all your filthiness: and I will cleanse you from all your idols. And I will give you a new heart and put a new spirit within you: and I will take away the stony heart out of your flesh and will give you a heart of flesh. And I will put my spirit in the midst of you." And Zachariah (9): "And he shall speak peace to the Gentiles and his power shall be from sea to sea, and from the rivers even to the ends of the earth... And the Lord their God will save them in that day, as the flock of his people: for holy stones shall be lifted up over his land. For what is the good thing of him, and what is his beautiful thing, but the corn of the elect and wine bringing forth virgins?"

Indeed it is plain enough, for us who read the Prophets now, that there was to be a spiritualization at every point: even at the point of priesthood and sacrifice where Israel had most scrupulously observed the Law. For the Jewish priests and the Jewish sacrifices were but figures of, and preparations for, something that was mysteriously to transcend them. The Messiah was to be (Ps. 109) "a priest forever according to the order of Melchizedek"—a strange phrase, for Melchizedek, who had offered a sacrifice of bread and wine, was not a Jew. As for the priesthood, so for the sacrifices: "From the rising of the sun even to the going down, my name is great among the Gentiles: and in every place there is sacrifice and there is offered to my name a clean oblation. For my name is great among the Gentiles saith the Lord of hosts" (Mal. 1:11).

Everything in Israel was preparatory, looked forward to something which should complete it. The Law given by God to Moses was not a consummation. It was a preparation: a hard and heavy preparation: not maturity, but a superb training for maturity.

F. J. SHEED

NARRATIVE

I

In the fifteenth year of the reign of Tiberius Caesar, says St. Luke —the year 27 A.D.—John the Baptist began such a whirlwind preaching campaign as Israel had never known. He was that John, son of Mary's cousin Elizabeth, whose birth was announced by the Angel Gabriel five or six months before Christ's, who was to be filled with the Holy Ghost from his mother's womb, who was to go before the Lord, as St. Luke tells us; who was not the Light but was to give testimony of the Light, as St. John tells us. He exhorted all Israel to penance and baptized multitudes; but, when men thought he might be the Christ, he insisted that the Christ was to come and was to baptize them with a baptism mightier than his. To John came Jesus, then about thirty, demanding to be baptized: and after His baptism the Holy Ghost descended as a dove upon Him, and a voice came from Heaven: "Thou art my beloved Son, in whom I am well pleased."

Immediately upon His baptism, Jesus was led by the Holy Ghost into the desert, where He spent forty days in prayer and fasting; was tempted by Satan and vanquished him; began to gather disciples; and at a wedding in Cana, a few miles from Nazareth, performed His first public miracle and so ended His hidden life—at the request of His mother He changed water into wine.

From Galilee where all this happened, Jesus went to Jerusalem and there did the one thing that would mean that everyone in Palestine to the smallest child would hear of Him—He drove the money-changers from the Temple. Still in Judea, He had the conversation with the Pharisee Nicodemus in which He told of the baptism He would institute—"unless a man be born again of water and the Holy Ghost, he shall not enter into the Kingdom of Heaven," as well as of the death He would die—"As Moses lifted up the serpent in the desert, so must the Son of Man be lifted up."

II

WITH the arrest of John the Baptist by Herod Antipas—who ultimately slew him—Jesus left Judea to open His own ministry in Galilee, lingering a little in Samaria on the way. In Galilee He healed a ruler's son, preached in His own town of Nazareth but established His abode in Capharnaum, by the Lake of Tiberias (the other name for the Sea of Galilee), probably in the house of Simon, a fisherman, whose name He changed to Peter, Rock. His ministry proper had begun. He preached, of penance and the coming of the Kingdom, and worked miracle upon miracle—including the miraculous haul of fish which was followed by the definitive call of Peter, James and John to join themselves to Him.

By now the opposition was beginning to take shape. At Capharnaum He healed a paralytic but first forgave his sins, which led to an accusation of blasphemy. He called to Him a tax-gatherer (who was to be the apostle Matthew) and in his house sat at table with Matthew's disreputable friends—which led to an accusation of moral laxity, and unfavorable comparison with the rigidly ascetical life of John the Baptist and his followers. Then there were problems about the Sabbath—His followers plucked ears of corn on that day, and He Himself healed a man with a withered hand. He answered their complaints unanswerably. And He claimed to be Lord of the Sabbath. Thus early, Pharisees and Herodians, so ill-assorted allies, began to plan for His destruction.

Then comes one of the decisive things—the Sermon on the Mount. It was preceded by a whole night "passed in the prayer of God," after which He made the definite choice of twelve to be His apostles. Then the crowds thronged, not only from Galilee where He was, but from Judea, from Jerusalem itself, and from Tyre and Sidon on the Mediterranean coast. He healed the sick—"distressed with pain and sickness of every sort, the possessed, the lunatics, the palsied." Then He went up into a mountain, and the most famous of all sermons began. First, the Beatitudes—Blessed are the poor in spirit, the meek, those who mourn, who hunger and thirst after righteousness, the merciful, the peacemakers, all who are persecuted for God's sake. Then a great body of moral and ascetical teaching, exalting love but giving stern warning of Hell for the un-loving. Much of His moral teaching is a restatement and interiorization of the law of Moses. He had come not to destroy the law but to fulfill it: but the formula He used—"Moses said to you.... But I say to you"—claimed a superiority to the Law that stunned his hearers more even than His claims to be Lord of the Sabbath.

Back in Capharnaum He healed the servant of a Roman officer, whose phrase "Lord I am not worthy that thou shouldst enter under my roof" is enshrined in our Eucharistic liturgy. At Naim he raised a widow's dead son to life. The discussions and dissensions about Him went on. His fame grew but the doubts grew too. John the Baptist in prison sent disciples to Him to reassure themselves; the Pharisees were furious that He allowed a harlot to anoint His feet; some of His relations thought He was mad. But the travelling and the teaching went on all over Galilee. We have come to the time of the first great group of parables—of the Sower, the Seed growing secretly, the Cockle, the Mustard Seed, the Leaven, the Treasure hid in a field and the Pearl of great price, the Net, and the Householder—in which the nature of His Kingdom begins to emerge, a spiritual Kingdom, not that earthly one of the Jewish hope.

Capharnaum is on the west of the Lake of Galilee. After six or seven months there, He brought His teaching and healing to the eastern shore—there most notably He allowed unclean spirits driven from a man to enter a herd of swine. Back in Galilee comes what must surely be one of the agonizing moments of His life—He preached in His own town of Nazareth. His own people rejected Him and tried to kill Him: not altogether surprisingly, since He had talked of times when God had favoured Gentiles rather than Jews.

Once more He crossed the lake and went to a desert place near Bethsaida. A crowd of five thousand followed Him: there was the, by now almost routine, teaching and healing: and towards the end of a day in which none had eaten, Jesus fed the crowd by a miraculous multiplication of five loaves and two fishes. Out of this miracle, He drew the teaching given in the synagogue at Capharnaum, and set out by St. John in his sixth chapter, of Himself as the Bread of Life—"Unless you eat the flesh of the Son of Man and drink his blood you can not have life in you. The man who eats my flesh and drinks my blood enjoys eternal life, and I will raise him up at the last day. My flesh is real food, my blood is real drink. He who eats my flesh and drinks my blood lives in me and I in him." It was too much even for many of His disciples, who simply left Him: but the Twelve remained with Him.

The best part of a year had passed since Jesus had taken up His abode in Capharnaum. Now He went to Jerusalem for Pentecost, infuriated the Jews further by healing a paralyzed man on the Sabbath, accusing them of unfaithfulness to Moses and making a frightening claim for Himself—"all men should honour the Son as they honour the Father." But He did not stay in Judea, for they sought to kill Him and He had much yet to do. So He taught again in Galilee, where scribes and Pharisees followed Him from Jerusalem to question Him, but could hardly have enjoyed the experience; went to the sea-coast cities of Tyre and Sidon and back to Galilee, once again fed a crowd, four thousand this time, by a miraculous multiplication of food.

St. Peter and the other apostles were with Him in these goings and comings and had already been entrusted with a teaching and healing mission of their own. Their faith had been tested hard by the teaching that they must eat His flesh and drink His blood, but with one exception they were still wholly His, yet with no clearness in their own minds whether or not He might be the Messiah, whether or not He might be human or more than human or divine. They were sure of one thing only: that He had the words of eternal life: and they had one strong hope, that when He founded the Kingdom He talked of so much, they would hold high rank in it.

To us, reading in the light of all that has happened, their slowness of comprehension seems beyond comprehension.

Now at least Jesus made a more determined effort to clarify their minds—about Himself, themselves and His Kingdom.

At Caesarea Philippi, in the north of Galilee, He drew from Peter the confession that He was the Christ, the Son of the living God—which is at least an assertion that Jesus is the Messiah, and (given all they had heard Our Lord say of His equality with the Father) surely an assertion of His divinity. Jesus met Peter's confession with the announcement that He would build His Church upon Peter, who must have found the next series of events a little dazing. He has just heard that he is to be the head of Christ's Kingdom on earth—think what that meant to a Jew with the thousand-year expectation of the Kingdom, raised to a new power by a year or more of constant companionship with a Messiah beyond any Old Testament dream. Within a few minutes, he hears Christ warn the apostles of His own coming suffering and death and hears himself called Satan—the tempter—by Christ for urging Him not to undergo so much agony and infamy. The week that followed could hardly have been long enough to lift the pain and fear and humiliation from Peter's mind: but at the end of it Christ raised him once more to the heights—spiritually, of course, but physically too. For He took Peter and James and John into a high mountain—Tabor probably—and there was transfigured before them, the glory that was ever His being allowed for that brief while to shine through and be seen of men. With the Transfiguration Jesus' ministry in Galilee is really at an end.

On their way back to Capharnaum, He once more tells of the suffering and death that must come to Him, adding the grim detail that He is to be betrayed, and the explicit statement that on the third day He will rise again. There is now a great mass of teaching, directed it would seem at the apostles, forming them for the work they must do: culminating in the injunction that we must forgive not seven times but till seventy times seven.

III

FROM now, Jesus is in Judea, where His death is planned and certain. In Jerusalem the scribes and Pharisees ply Him with questions, and His answers leave no place for compromise. When they bring Him the woman taken in adultery, He challenges any man who is sinless to throw the first stone. He speaks more and more clearly of His own divinity. He heals a man born blind and the Pharisees hold a full-scale investigation. He tells a lawyer, set upon knowing whether all the two hundred forty-eight commands and three hundred sixty-five prohibitions of the Law were of the same rank, that there is a first and a second among them, that the two great commands are to love God wholly and love our neighhour as ourself. In the parable of the Good Samaritan He rejects Jewish exclusiveness wholly. But His own main interest, perhaps, is in the formation of His followers. He gives to Martha and Mary at Bethany the great lesson that contemplation is the higher and holier state; and upon a disciple's request that He teach them how to pray, He gives us the Lord's Prayer.

The Pharisees continued importunate: suggested that He cast out devils by diabolic power. He answered their hostility with a great storm of denunciation, and they were set more implacably than ever in their determination to destroy Him. When, in response to their irritated question "How long dost thou hold our souls in suspense: if thou be the Christ tell us plainly," He answered, "I and the Father are one," they took up stones to stone Him. But He would not let them slay Him yet. He crossed over the Jordan and there for a while remained. To this period belong another great mass of parables—of the Banquet, the Great Supper, the Lost Sheep and the Lost Coin—which seem clearly enough to say that the Jews have forfeited their priority: then the parables of the Prodigal Son, and of Dives and Lazarus which underline the same truth unmistakably: as do the parables of the Pharisee and the Publican and the Labourers in the Vineyard which came soon after. One cannot be certain of the order of events just here. There is the healing of the ten lepers (with only the Samaritan returning to give thanks) and a magnificent body of teaching on the Second Coming and the Last Judgment, on the providence of God, on riches and poverty, on marriage and virginity, on the necessity of becoming as little children.

The determination of His enemies to destroy Him was given its last edge of sharpness by a miracle He worked at

Bethany—He raised the four-day-dead Lazarus, brother of Martha and Mary, to life. A miracle of that magnitude, and only a mile or two from Jerusalem itself, was too much: "If we let him alone, all will believe in him and the Romans will come and take away our place and nation." Jesus retired for a little while to Ephrem, some fifteen miles away. It was noted that He did not come up to Jerusalem before the Pasch: and orders were given that anyone who knew where He was should give information: He must be left no more at liberty.

It could only be a matter of days now, as He knew. He gave His apostles the most detailed foretelling of His betrayal and scourging and death, but also of His resurrection.

LÉONCE DE GRANDMAISON, S.J.

THE SITUATION IN PALESTINE

St. Luke tells us that John the Baptist began his preaching in "the fifteenth year of the reign of Tiberius Caesar, Pontius Pilate being governor of Judaea, and Herod being tetrarch of Galilee, and Philip his brother tetrach of Ituraea and the country of Trachonitis, and Lysanius tetrach of Abilina: under the high priests Annas and Caiaphas (Luke 3:1–2). This medley of names, titles and duties warns us from the start that we have to deal with a complex state of affairs. The fact is that the political unity re-established in Palestine by Herod the Idumaean at the cost of an atrocious war of three years' duration (40–37 B.C.) had been again broken down. This half-Jew, crafty and cruel, who was to complete his reign with the massacre of the Innocents, did at least enforce order and obtained, even if he did not merit it, the name of "the Great." He reigned from 37 to 4 B.C.

In his time the Temple was magnificently rebuilt, peace was maintained, the pride of the sacerdotal families was humbled, and the marked hellenism of the prince, together with his constant devotion to the more powerful of the Romans, was limited by a sure instinct for the critical point beyond which Jewish endurance would give place to despair and revolt. The dark intrigues of the palace and the unforgivable murders which blackened the last years of the reign did not prevent Augustus from ratifying the chief features of the Idumaean's will. This divided his land between his three surviving sons—he had put to death his three elder sons. By this will, Archelaus received Judaea; Herod Antipas (who beheaded John the Baptist and appears in the story of the Passion) was given Galilee and Peraea; while Ituraea and the north-eastern districts went to Philip.

By the year 30 only the last two retained their dominions. In Judaea (properly so-called) Archelaus made himself so unpopular that his subjects forwarded to Rome a petition against him. Augustus received it in A.D. 6 and in consequence placed the province directly under a Roman magistrate, who was a mere procurator (we should call him a Lieutenant-Governor) of the Pro-consul of Syria, and resided on the coast at Caesarea, whence communication with Rome was none too easy. His habitual absence from Jerusalem, to which he went every year with a strong escort at the time of the Feast of the Passover, together with the care taken by the Romans to leave to subject peoples a portion or a shadow of autonomy, meant that the high council of the nation, the Sanhedrin, which had been almost abolished during Herod's reign, regained a certain amount of independence. Composed of seventy-one members, "princes of the priests" (chiefs of the principal families of sacerdotal caste), "scribes" (doctors expert in the interpretation of the Law), and "elders" (senators) the Sanhedrin was presided over at great functions by the high priest. In the time of Jesus, this tribunal was in actual fact the sole Jewish authority in matters political and religious....

We see in the Judaea of those days, less perhaps than elsewhere, but in the same way, rich and poor, "the great ones of the flesh" and the small, persons of quality and the populace. As always happens, the first class are the better known to us: it is they who, in very great measure, make history, and it is always they who write it. And it is chiefly with them that we are concerned in this chapter. But if we were to forget the others we should run the danger of not understanding the Gospels, and it is the Gospels which offer us the most vivid pictures of these. Leisured artisans, and fishermen who could be more easily detached from their boats than labourers could be uprooted from their soil, the apostles of Jesus almost all belonged to that little world of true Israelites, without guile and without artifice, formed on the model made familiar to us by the Wisdom literature and the Psalms.

The Master praised them in the person of Nathaniel (John 1:47) and, which is much more, he called them to him. Jewish scholars who strive to explain and to diminish the contrast between the Gospel and the Pharisaic ideal, locate the difference in the fact that, far from repulsing these men as incapable of sharing in the Kingdom of God, Jesus opened the door wide to them. He went lower than that, even to sinners and publicans, but chiefly he talked familiarly and in friendly fashion with the ignorant, the rude, and "this accursed multitude which knoweth not the law" (John 7:49).

Above these masses of the people we find, ruling them or at least distinct from them, at this period in Judaea, "the rich and prudent" whose importance was assured to them by their birth, fortune and knowledge of the Law.

The *Herodians* are three times mentioned in the Gospels (Mark 3:6; 12:13; Matt. 22:16). Without constituting a particular sect, analogous to those which will be described below, these politicians, who were resigned to the Roman rule, and were devoted to or rallied to the power of the Idumaean princes, were recruited from the families which the state of affairs existing under the Herods had not too much offended or injured, they saw in this government a more or less tolerable middle term half-way between total subjection to the Empire and an independence which they no longer believed to be possible. The words spoken at the meeting of the Sanhedrin about the miracles and increasing popularity of Jesus express very fairly the timid wisdom of the Herodians and the proximity of Rome which made them desire, and almost love, the scarcely national dynasty of the Herods.

At the other extremity of the political rainbow, a turbulent, fanatical group, the *Zealots,* were jealous observers of the Law, and, as such, were Pharisees and no more. What enabled Josephus to distinguish them from the main body of the Pharisees was the fact that, being before all else nationalists, the Zealots were the declared enemies of all foreign domination. Already formed in Gospel times, this turbulent minority increased as a consequence of the troubles which followed the ephemeral reign of Herod Agrippa I, who died in 44. It fomented and fanned the successive revolts which led to the capture and sack of Jerusalem in 70.

The *Essenes,* who are known only through occasional (though detailed and friendly) passages in Philo, Josephus and Pliny the Elder, have greatly aroused the curiosity of scholars and have driven not a few amateur historians to delirium. They formed cenobitical groups, freely recruited, and their chief centres were situated around the Dead Sea. According to Josephus they numbered as many as four thousand. Their origin is unknown: but traces of them are found possibly towards the middle, and certainly towards the end of the first century B.C. After undergoing a postulancy of one year, they were initiated and given a knife, a belt and a white robe. They kept themselves, worked with their hands, as a general rule preserved celibacy, did not keep slaves and did not engage in commerce.

As all goods were held in common, meals were taken together, with a grave and religious solemnity. Their scrupulous, concerted, almost ritualistic care of personal cleanliness, and their abstention from blood sacrifices, might make us think that the Essenes were very different from other Israelites.

In reality, they were (although following their own particular course) true Jews, faithful to the fundamental beliefs of Judaism, strict observers of the Law, and especially of the Sabbatarian precepts, great readers of the Holy Books, who sent their offerings regularly to the Temple at Jerusalem. If Schürer goes too far in calling them "decided Pharisees" (for their faith seems rather to have turned towards the immortality of the soul than to the resurrection of the body), if certain characteristics seem to betray foreign origin and discipline (possibly Greek or Pythagorean, more probably Iranian), the Essenes remain for all essentials within the religious body of Israel. In any case, nothing could differ more from primitive Christianity, which could at the most see in them an example, when for some time it put into practice at Jerusalem the common holding of property. In other respects, that is to say in almost all its characteristics (its rigid legalism, its scrupulous attention to corporal and saving purifications, its moral rigorism extending normally to prohibition of marriage, and its aloofness from all that was sinful, common or profane), the Order was absolutely contrary to the spirit and the habits of Jesus. It could be more justly asked whether certain of the Master's criticisms were not aimed at the refinements and exclusiveness of the Essenes…

Let us come to the great parties, which were opponents and rivals on many points, but which a common interest could partially draw together and unite against Jesus: the *Sadducees* and the *Pharisees*. The distant origin of these sects has been sought for in their conflicting tendencies, the one rigidly Jewish, the other more open to foreign influences, which divided the Jewish leaders throughout the period which followed the return from exile in the middle of the sixth century.

At first the severe tendency, closed to all compromise, which was favoured by the leaders of the migration, Ezra and Nehemiah, and by the fact that the greater number of the social leaders of the people had remained in Mesopotamia, undoubtedly reigned supreme. It is the period of the *Soferim*, i.e., the commentators on the book *par excellence*, the *Sefer-ha-torah* (book of the Law). Promulgated again among this group of devout Jews, the Law became truly the *form* of this people, in the Aristotelian sense of the word, the intimate regulator of its life, its specific principle of order and of hierarchy. In it was sought every rule for public and private organisation, every solution for the extremely complex cases which were raised by the return to Judaea of the caravans from Persia, coming as they were amongst a scattered population of pagan or semi-pagan occupiers. From this necessity there sprang the important occupation of the scribe, the commentator on the sole rule of God. Sprung generally from modest origins, often laymen, though not always (Ezra himself was of the sacerdotal caste), the scribes favoured with all their power whatever tended to separate Israel from the people amongst whom they lived, with the object of restoring an autonomous state. Mixed marriages, therefore, intercourse with pagans or the semi-Jews of Samaria, and anything approaching idolatry, were zealously denounced.

On the other hand, some of the most important of the priests who had returned from exile, pastors and leaders of the people in this theocracy in which the two powers were confounded, remained in contact with the Persian authorities, and even went so far as to unite themselves in marriage with influential families not of pure Jewish race. Such was the case, for example, of the high priest Eliasib: he was united to the family of Tobias the Ammonite, and one of his grandsons, the son of Joiadah (and therefore the son and grandson of high priests) married a daughter of Sanaballat the Horonite. And Tobias and Sanaballat, sworn enemies of Nehemiah, opposed with all their might the rebuilding of the walls of Jerusalem undertaken by the latter.

We can see in these two tendencies, the one aristocratic and liberal, represented by the high sacerdotal caste, and the other more humble and rigidly closed to all foreign influence, an anticipation of the future.

Yet the origin of the parties of the Sadducees and Pharisees does not go back so far; it must be sought in the obscure period which separates the end of the era of the scribes and the death of Simon the Just from the brutal attempt of Antiochus Epiphanes to Hellenise the country (roughly 270–175 B.C.).

Then was completely shattered the unity of the sacerdotal and learned oligarchy, the legendary "Great Synagogue" of later Jewish tradition, which maintained on the whole for two centuries, despite varying fortunes, a certain general understanding amongst those faithful to the Law. Whatever form that assembly may have had (and we must not be too quick to see in it the features of the future Sanhedrin), it united the double authority of the great priestly families and the doctors (priests or laymen) who gave the people from day to day the interpretation of the Law. The members of the first group, who were the more rigid the more liberty they took for themselves, and were satisfied with a literalism which cut short all casuistical discussion, stood theoretically, if not practically, for the written Law without gloss. The others strove to give to the sacred texts a flexibility which would enable them to be adapted to a change of circumstances; this they sought to do by the double means of a subtle exegesis of the letter of the law, and a traditional interpretation, a kind of oral law, which later took form in the Mishna. It was probably on that point that the separation took place.

From whichever side the initiative came, the somewhat ill-sounding name of the *Separated* (*peruchim*, Pharisees) was applied to those who abandoned the high authorities of the Temple. Thus it was indicated that they formed a body apart and were seceders. They themselves did not call themselves by this name, but preferred that of *haberim* (colleagues, companions, fellow-workers). But the other name prevailed, and it is as Pharisees that all ancient tradition knew them. In contradistinction to them, and before political circumstances led them to reintroduce certain Pharisees into the supreme council of the nation, the representatives of the priestly caste were called or called themselves the sons of Sadoc (Sadducees), in allusion no doubt to a prince of the priests of the time of David and Solomon, Sadoc, whose real or fictitious descendents were regarded as the sacerdotal family *par excellence.*

Each party was wedded to its own opinions, while the mass of the people, naturally closer to the Pharisees, oscillated between currents which sometimes came near to intermingling, only speedily to resume their separate and often antagonistic courses. The Sadducees were ambitious, and consequently opportunist, very tolerant in the matter of alliances, understandings, and compromises with pagans and half-Jews, hard towards the poorer people; they were unscrupulous in increasing their personal fortunes from the enormous contributions of money and other offerings which flowed into the Temple from all parts of the Holy Land and from the Dispersion, but they professed an unswerving conservatism in matters of the Law. They reduced the whole of Revelation, at least all that was of absolute authority, to the five books of Moses, rejecting or disputing, as illegitimate or imaginary, more recently developed beliefs on the resurrection of the body, the world of spirits, and the Messianic Kingdom. The Law alone, and in its strict letter, was of weight with them. It was less as priests (many of the priests were Pharisees) than as aristocrats and leaders of a dominant faction, as interpreters of Revelation and of the Law, that this minority, full of haughtiness towards the lowly, and bending only to the great, stood in opposition to the Pharisees. These men, well-born and endowed with worldly goods, looked with jealousy on the progress of a caste formed outside themselves, and criticised their adversaries as innovators and rebels. They deplored the growing prestige brought to the Pharisees by their zeal, their knowledge, and their rigorism. They found these casuists an obstacle and an embarrassment.

But we should not imagine that the whole Sadducean party was of the type stigmatised by the Talmud:

> "*House of Boethus? Woe is me!*
> *Woe is me by reason of their bludgeons.*
> *House of Annas? Woe is me!*
> *Woe is me by reason of their viperish hissings.*
> *House of Cantharos? Woe is me!*
> *Woe is me by reason of their calumnies.*
> *House of Ismael, sons of Phabi? Woe is me!*
> *Woe is me by reason of their clenched hands.*
> *They are high priests, their sons are treasurers, their*

> *sons-in-law are inspectors of the Temple, and their footmen belabour the people with clubs."*

We must not judge the whole party by the radically exclusive members, and the insolently secular attitude of the families which monopolised the office of high priest. Scholars are inclined to see in the *Ecclesiasticus* of Jesus the son of Sirach a book that is representative of the primitive Sadducees; from this we should have to conclude that the sect had a theology of its own, though very conservative in nature, and that it treated the prophets with honour, if it did not put them on a level with the five books of the Law....

As opposed to the Essenes, dreamers absorbed in moral and ritual matters, and the Sadducees, aristocrats by race and politicians by instinct, the "Companions" (*haberim*), the "Devout" (*chasidim*)—who soon came to be called the Pharisees and have remained such for us—formed a party which was before all things religious and national, a kind of Holy League, the Jewish party pure and simple. Their whole aim was in the first place to purge the people of God who had returned to the Promised Land, from foreign infiltrations and influence, and then to preserve them from the aggressive, cunning and sometimes (as in the time of the Seleucidae) violent propaganda of surrounding paganism. In this defence of the Jewish spirit and customs, the essential wall or, to use a metaphor dear to the rabbis, the protecting hedge of Jahweh's vine, was the Law of Moses. Recruited from all classes of society, including the most humble, without distinction of priests and laity, and counting among their number the majority of the intellectuals, scribes and doctors, the Pharisees were thus before all the men of the Law: its interpreters, its avengers, and at need its martyrs. St. Paul, when he wishes to express his passionate attachment to the Law, is content to say: "An Hebrew of the Hebrews. *According to the law, a Pharisee*" (Phil. 3:5). In saying that, he says all.

In their absolute trust in the Torah, some inclined to make it independent, to some extent, even of God. The little collection called *The Sentences of the Fathers*, which represents Pharisaism in its most authentic aspect, and gives us the best of it for the period reaching from the first century B.C. to the end of the second century A.D., practically identifies the scribe with the saint: knowledge of the Law sanctifies after the manner of a sacrament. Rabbi Meir (about 135) said: "Everyone who gives himself to the study of the Torah for its own sake is worthy of every good. What is more, the whole world and its fulness is not worth more than he."

In these thoroughly religious pages God is scarcely named. The Law takes up all the space, because, for a Pharisee, it virtually signifies the whole of divine truth, so far as it is accessible to the human mind. And they had for it the respect that is due to God: the most innocent distraction during the study of the Torah is culpable, as being one which interrupts a prayer.

Rabbi Jacob (who died in 175) said: "If a man walks about while studying [the Torah] and interrupts his study to say 'How beautiful is that tree,' or 'How beautiful is that wild spot,' Scripture holds such words to be a sin which makes his soul guilty."

In this way the Pharisee drew from the Law the rules for the whole conduct of his life, private and public. This last fact, which endowed the scribe with the very power of the State, was bound to lead to conflicts with the political powers. And in fact neither the Hasmonaean princes from the time of John Hyrcanus, excluding the personal reign of the old Queen Alexandra (78–69 B.C.), nor the Idumaeans accepted this tutelage. But whether favoured or suspected, sometimes even persecuted, the *Separated* never ceased to be feared by reason of their power with the people. This power, which Josephus states, with obvious exaggeration, to have been practically unlimited, was certainly great and often preponderant. It was based in great part on the manner in which the Pharisees had decentralised and in a certain sense laicised and democratised the religion of Israel. The Temple remained its centre; the hegemony of the great priestly families, and especially of the high priest, continued to be exercised; but even there, in the Temple, the Pharisees had their influence, and had caused daily prayers to be established, and instituted a sort of delegation of pious laity representing the people of Israel at the daily sacrifice. Outside the temple, by means of the synagogue and worship in the home, they had severed the line which bound the whole religion of the people to the Temple. The rabbi and the father of the family tended more and more to supplant the Levite and the priest. Finally, in matters casuistical and the application of the Law to daily life by means of subtle exegeses and traditional interpretation, a sort of unwritten Law commenting upon the written one—in these matters the Pharisees were supreme, and for an Israelite desirous of devoutly fulfilling his duties, indispensable. Women especially (as Josephus noted) looked upon them as their oracle.

Less dependent than the chosen priesthood on political vicissitudes, less entangled than the Zealots in militant xenophobia, the bulk of the Pharisees represented, from the time of the Maccabees to the fall of Jerusalem, the kernel of Israel, the heart of Judaism by their ardour in observing, imposing and explaining the Law, by their minute knowledge, which though literal and rigid was yet real, by the hold which their puritanism gave them over the people, and by the religious feeling which made them favour the more purified and spiritual doctrines.

So, too, it was through the *Separated* that the Jewish people survived the appalling catastrophes of the first and second centuries. The barriers established, or re-erected, around the race; the traditions jealously maintained within these closed groups; the supple resistance which gave way only in order to obtain; the political opportunism which bowed to every *de facto* government to snatch from each of them toleration and the maximum of possible concessions; the enormous mass of sayings, prescriptions, decisions, and recollections which crystallised into the two Talmuds: all these are the work of the Pharisees. And it is sufficient to read the Gospels to see the preponderant part played by them in the opposition encountered by Christ.

This very opposition makes impartiality more difficult for the Christian historian towards the principal enemies of Jesus. But he himself has plainly taught us that truth alone delivers. And while proving that they became by their blind obstinacy and the malice of their leaders the enemies of the Kingdom of God, we willingly acknowledge that the Pharisees played a useful and sometimes a glorious part during the century and a half which preceded our era. Those who spied upon Jesus were the descendants, buried in the formalism of the Law, and sometimes poisoned by sterile pride, of the great men who had freed Israel from the yoke of the Gentiles at the price of their blood. All that was best in the literature which preceded the advent of Christ bore as a rule the imprint of the beliefs, the hopes, and the passions which were theirs. And even in the time of the Saviour, an impressive minority did not sin against the light. In this matter the *Acts of the Apostles* are very helpful in completing the testimony borne by the Gospels. They show us in the youthful Church a great number of recruits from the party of the Pharisees; beginning with St. Paul, they were not the most unimportant.

In conclusion we must note that, while stigmatizing their merciless literalism, their complacent casuistry and their pride, Jesus aimed much more at the vices of conduct, the abuse of holy things, the canonization of human tradition, the ill-inspired zeal of the *Separated,* than at their doctrinal position. On the characteristic questions of the resurrection of the body, the existence and the action of spiritual forces, the Master was in agreement with them. Nor did he disdain to employ (though moderately) their exegetical methods. He acknowledged their relative authority in the domain of the interpretation of the Law: "The Scribes and Pharisees have sitten on the chair of Moses. All things therefore whatsoever they say to you, observe and do: but according to their works do ye not" (Matt. 23:2–3).

THE BOOK OF THE SAVIOUR ❧ VOLUME TWO

HILAIRE BELLOC

❧ ❧

CAPHARNAUM AND THE LAKE

He makes but a false picture of those supreme three years during which the Godhead created the Catholic Church, if he imagine them to have been passed amid a pastoral and simple people of the more debased oriental sort, such as we find for the most part in that desolate countryside today.

The scene of the Gospels and, in particular this lake of Tiberias, which was the nucleus of all that went before the Passion, the stage on which or from which doctrine and revelation were proclaimed, was, in Our Lord's day, a scene of greatness, wealth and splendour; of high civilisation and of man by his creative power adding all that he could add to nature.

Where there were so many rich there were many, many more of the poor; but the world in which Our Lord and His Apostles moved, the surroundings of all that story—of the teaching from the boat, of the Transfiguration, of the Sermon on the Mount, of the casting out of devils and of that turning point, the confession of St. Peter—was a world which, to the eye and to the ear and to all the senses of those who passed through its thronged porticoes, was a high and exalted world, comparable to, but far more dignified than, the wealthy centres of today in our teeming western Europe.

Its civilisation was Greek. That civilisation was superimposed upon an older population, mainly Jewish in faith (though largely also Pagan), Semitic in tongue but in dress presumably and in general habit much what the rest of the Mediterranean people were. The dress was *not* what the Arab dress is today: *not* the modern Oriental garments in which it is still fashionable to represent Our Lord and His Apostles.

Stand on the high land to the north and east of the little shore plain of Genesareth, and look down those few miles of water, eight miles across at their broadest stretch. You see the lake narrowing down to the southward, the high hills closing round about it, forbidding to the left and to the right; at the extreme end of your view the lump of land on which lay Gadara, and the opening of that oppressive trench, deep dug below the level of the Mediterranean, the Jordan valley. Here and there you see a few new houses springing up, much more rarely the ruins, often but a stone or two, of something older; empty wastes of reed on the flat shores and some way off on the western bank, the only agglomeration which seems worthy of a name, rather a large ramshackle village than a city, still called in its degradation Tiberias, and still overhung by the dark rock on which was planted its citadel. For the rest, nothing. You are fortunate if you so much as see one sail on that flat, shining oval of water.

But in those old days it was a pageant. All round the shores of that inland water was a succession of fine towns, in an almost uninterrupted ring, passing one into the other as do those pleasure-places which we built today along the shores of the Channel, but how much more glorious!

Capharnaum was a great place, there to your right, where even now for three-quarters of a mile or more, its unhappy stones lie scattered upon the Galilean grass. Bethsaida, to your left upon the flat, where the upper Jordan pushes its delta into the north of the lake, had all the loveliness of Greece stamped upon it; and beyond again the string of white columns and walls in place after place along the eastern shore; in between and above them the groves of chestnut trees, on the heights the outlying Greek towns of the Decapolis.

On the extreme limit of your view, where the lake ceased, Tarichaeae, where the pickling of fish from the lake supported an industry which sent its delicacies all over the Roman world. Hidden between that point and the other great and noble town of Tiberias were the baths which the wealthy sought not only from all that country, but from far away, for their healing. Men counted nine towns at least, apart from intervening suburbs and villages, along that short ring of coastal land.

There in Capharnaum stood up the grandeur of the Great Synagogue, with its high Corinthian columns and the carving of the Manna in between.

It was in this building, majestic with the outward order of Greece, consecrated within by the traditions and teaching of those who had maintained for centuries the worship of the Most High God, that Our Lord first proclaimed the Eucharist.

There, in the Great Synagogue of Capharnaum, to its crowded hall, were these strange words first said: "I am the living bread which came down from heaven. If any man eat of this bread he shall live for ever: and the bread that I will give is my flesh for the life of the world..."

Those strange words were said, and they were bewildering. In the buzz of talk arising on this could be discerned such a protest as this: "How can this man give us his flesh to eat?" But the silence that followed was broken by the reiterated words: "Except you eat the flesh of the Son of Man and drink his blood you shall not have life in you."

If you turned, standing on that rising ground above the lake by Chorozain, and looked northward, you saw the snows of Hermon rising high into heaven nearly ten thousand feet above the lake, barely thirty miles away, and dominating all that land. On the flanks of that great mountain at its feet some twenty odd miles from where you stood, was the little paradise (as it then was) of Caesarea Philippi. There the living waters gushed out of the limestone with a wealth of greenery about them; the marble columns of a temple shone upon the cliff above, and the Greeks, delighting in so much beauty, dedicated the groves to Pan and to the Nymphs. Thence ran the great Roman road to Damascus.

It was here, in Caesarea Philippi, that loveliest corner of what was still then everywhere a lovely land, that the famous question was asked and answered: "Whom do you say that I am?" ... "Thou art Christ, the Son of the living God." And here it was that openly and by a solemn published word the indestructible title of the Catholic Church was proclaimed: "I will build my church and the gates of hell shall not prevail against it."

The site is symbolical. It is an origin in every way, is that very height of the Jordan valley. There stretch southward, past the lesser mere, then past the Sea of Galilee, then down the long trench to the Dead Sea, and the mass of bare stony heights which are Judea, all the scenes of this story. Thence runs for its hundred and thirty miles the countryside on which all the future of the world from that day onwards has turned.

And thence it was that Our Lord turning His lace southwards towards all that land, began His journey to that appointed end, to Jerusalem, to the Passion, and death upon the Cross.

Such was the setting of the story; such the kingdom of this world, as it moved past the Apostles in their goings back and forth with their Master; everywhere the might of a great culture and the splendour of its sculptured stones and the wealth of its commerce and the crowds of its superabundant people.

Stand on that same height and look around you today. There is nothing. Magdala, the City of Pleasure, drawn luxuriously along the shore, has utterly departed; a hut or two and a bush. Great Capharnaum is the scattered stones hidden in growth on which men dispute whether it was really there or no; Chorozain is a doubtful name, a wretched hamlet; a traditional low cliff may be, or is, the mark of what was once Gerasa. And Tiberias, itself once a high city with three miles of walls, might be any one of the squalid overgrown villages which the wreck of civilisation has left like flotsam behind it.

So utterly has the blight and devastation of the half-barbaric conqueror reduced this land that even the names of what was once so great have become obscure.

No story is more famous than that of the Gadarene swine—yet only now are men, quite recently, fairly assured (but not yet quite assured) that the spelling is erroneous; that the true place of the miracle was not Gadara at all—how could it have been six miles from the lake shore and cut off from it by the deep valley of the Yarmuk?—but rather Gerasa.

Men dispute on Bethsaida: stood it here or there? Caesarea Philippi is not; the excellent title which Greek fancy gave it the Place of Pan, Paneas—is preserved in Arabic corruption —"Banias," a fortress in ruins also; but of all the beauty and wealth that stood there, nothing.

The Decapolis to the east, the Greek cities, are (all save Damascus), a desolation; and the refrain perpetually recurring is the same everywhere—ruins... ruins... ruins.

THE LAKE

WHEN Our Lord left Nazareth and began His public predication, He went down first to the Sea of Galilee close at hand. There it was He began to choose the Apostles; there it was that the great story openly began.

On this account the Sea of Galilee (which is also called the Lake of Tiberias) has become the most famous sheet of water in the world.

Nazareth itself stands in the folds of rolling highlands which reach the height of from two to three thousand feet above the sea, the highlands of Galilee. These hills are the distinctive feature of the country, standing separate as they do from the stony hills of Judea to the south; and from them down to the lake shore (a matter as the crow flies of fifteen miles but by the new road of seventeen) is a drop of over two thousand feet, over grassy country with here and there a village, such as Cana of Galilee, within an easy walk of Nazareth, where Our Lord worked his first miracle.

The road goes on, still falling, past the broad sward of Hattin, where was fought one of the most important battles in history, the battle in which the Christians lost the Holy Land, seven hundred and fifty years ago. It continues, the valley of the Upper Jordan opening before it, and the deep hollow in which the Lake lies, its waters at last apparent before you and the dark steep hills beyond, which correspond upon the east of the Jordan trench to what the hills of Galilee are upon the west.

So at last, at the end of half a day downwards, you come to the shore at the place which gave the Sea of Galilee its Greek and Roman name: the town of Tiberias.

I know many others have spoken with enthusiasm of the beauty they found in this deep cup, buried between the opposing hills. It was not beauty which affected me when I saw it; the landscape is stern, and I will maintain of this great site as of all else southward, down to Bethlehem itself, of all else in this land save Nazareth, that it carried more air of tragedy than any other.

Mighty things were done, the greatest of spiritual victories and the triumph of the Resurrection at the end—but I can only believe that the Passion has chiefly imprinted itself upon all that land wherein Our Lord taught, gave the signs from Heaven, and suffered, at last, the Agony.

Though here, on this placid oval mirror of the Lake, placid save for those very sudden storms which rise and are gone sometimes in an hour, such storms as you always find in the enclosed waters of mountain lands, there is no name or spot recalling the mighty tragedy, yet that tragedy broods over it.

It was first the knowledge and personal experience, it was later, when that generation had died, the Faith of Christian men, that the tragedy was succeeded by glory. And doubtless, to a full vision, all this land, from happy Nazareth in the north to Bethlehem, three days' journey away to the south, is lit, as by a sudden sunrise, with the Resurrection. It should be so. But to me as I first looked on that landscape it was not so, and I think would not be so were I to return there a hundred times. Rather the solemnity as of a profound horror, the sombre silence of the hillsides that hang so awfully about it, were filled with a precognition of what was to come.

Here all the first wonders were wrought; here first from Magdala, a little northward along the shore, came the woman whose association with the story will be spoken of till the end of the world. Here were the multitudes who heard the voice, here, further to the north again, stood Capharnaum, which should be filled with memories of revelation, of the beginning of doctrine, of the appearance of the Kingdom of God, and with nothing else.

But we know, and not we alone, that all this was to fail very quickly in the eyes of the world. It was to last three years, it was to end in a local climax at Jerusalem; it was not to be of very great immediate fame; and the close was to be intolerable pain of body and the worst suffering of the expectant mind-jeers and tortures and a dreadful death. The land has not escaped the stamp of that Deicide.

I note also that as the world progressed in its gradual apostasy, as doctrine faded from its intelligence, and as the meaning of all that was here done was lost to it, so did what is called "the modern mind" begin to sentimentalise over the landscape of Judea, and particularly over these waters of the Lake: insisting upon, exaggerating beauty, when it should rather have had before it the awful business which transformed the world. And let me say this too—although I know I am here far from repeating what others have said whose eyes have fallen upon the sacred soil—there seems to me to be in a sense upon all the places of the Predication, the public life of Our Lord, and not only in Jerusalem, the living echo stamped upon it of the Lamentation which Jesus made over the walls of the city, foreseeing their destruction.

For Tiberias also, and all the places round about, bears that mood of desolation and ruin which fell upon the Holy Land when the lesser thing conquered the greater, and the men of the desert, with their new degraded heresy, swept over and destroyed the splendours inherited by Christendom from the old Pagan world, whence our civilisation came.

Tiberias was stately and splendid, with the Grecian column everywhere and the marble statuary and colonnades which you may still see overthrown, lying in ruins, of city after city from Palmyra in the desert to Petra in the far south. All that loveliness, all that dignity, has gone; and the squalor has replaced it which follows everywhere at last the sweep of the Islamic conquest.

Magdala has been wiped out; a few stones and a house or two of no presence, a tree or two, and the reeds along the lake are all that remain. On the slope above stand the new villas of wealthy immigrant Jews. Capharnaum is not even a name. The Greek proportion and beauty, the Roman soldiery and order, the full life and wealth of that countryside, with its capital called after and, as it were, dedicated to the glory of the Empire and its head—all these have gone. And that feeling which oppresses every man who goes eastward of the Adriatic comes upon one almost fiercely here on these desolating shores.

Yet in the midst of all this, appearing visionary above the physical emptiness of what was once so active and so filled, moves the profound pageantry of the opening Gospel. Here were the words first said (in Aramaic, it is believed, to the poorer people, but surely in Greek to many) which were the prelude. Their strength gives substance to the deserted places, and peoples the shore and the slopes above.

If you look eastward over the water you see within you the stilling of the storm, and also the figure passing swiftly over the water to the astonished fishermen upon the boat. That boat, which was the poor possession of Cephas, called also Peter, is a vessel which can never founder, which shall not be cast upon a beach in age and broken up, as other vessels are.

The Sea of Galilee is today bereft of life and filled with its presence. It is empty to the eye and silent to the ear, but a multitude fills it, and the splendour of palaces and temples, many cities, wealth, the noise of soldiers, and in that setting the unique and novel gem, on that field the sowing of the seed; on that platform the foundation of the Church.

THE BOOK OF THE SAVIOUR ↭ VOLUME TWO

WALTER FARRELL, O.P.

↭ ↭

MINISTRY IN GALILEE

God came to teach men truth and to free them from sin; so He came to the places where truth was threatened and sin flourished. He elbowed His way into the crowded market-place, walked the dusty roads, thundered against the violation of the Temple at the very height of a feast. He did not sit back content with His perfection and graciously stooping to forgive any sinners who might come to Him. He went out on the highways and byways seeking the sinners, pursuing them like the Hound of Heaven He was, eagerly, anxiously, relentlessly.

He came that through Him we might have easy access to God. We needed His help, for it is not an easy thing to go to God, particularly when we are weighed down with sin; even though we know there is no place else to go, we still have our human pride and our human fear. The enemies of Christ unwittingly made clear to the sinners of all future ages what confidence and courage His familiar life with men had poured into the human hearts of His time by accusing Him of surrounding Himself with sinners and publicans. Sinners ever since have laughed with joy to learn that the men who had the most reason for terror were precisely the ones who came to the feet of the Son of God.

Of course they came to Christ; He had made Himself one with men. He did not embrace the rigid fasting and penance of John the Baptist, for He did not wish to tower above men, striking terror into their hearts; rather He came down among men that they might more easily walk into His divine heart. He gave a perfect example in the absolutely necessary things, and among these rigid abstinence from food and drink is not included. Abstinence is not an end in itself but a means by which men might attain to control and continence; the sinless Christ had no need of this means, so He lived as other men, eating and drinking.

All through His life, Christ felt the privations and tasted the joys of poverty. On His own testimony, He was hungry, thirsty, and without a place whereon to lay His head. Nor was this a condemnation of riches. It was no secret in Christ's time that riches can be an occasion of pride and offer opportunities for sins that are not open to the poor man; but then neither were the men of that time ignorant of the fact that poverty can be no less an occasion of sin, indeed, an occasion of all those sins a man will commit to seize the riches upon which his heart is set. It is neither riches nor poverty that count; but the poverty of spirit which is a casting aside of the trinkets of the world in the realization of how little they contribute to the perfection of man's life.

Men do not need riches for human living; they simply cannot get along without fellowship and law. It is small wonder that Christ insisted so strongly on these two. He came to perfect the imperfect law, yet His observance of that imperfect one was most exact; He came to liberate men from the burdens of the Old Law, but first He carried the burden Himself. None of His contemporaries could accuse Him of sin. He was no lawbreaker; for He would not have us miss the fact that the fruits of sin are degradation, subjection, and tyranny, not the liberty and perfection He came to give us. Even His indignant declaration that the Son of Man was Lord of the Sabbath was not a rejection of law but a condemnation of misinterpretation and vicious perversion of law. Clearly the law of the Sabbath was not meant to forbid divine works; it did not prohibit the works necessary for life, even for corporal life; above all, it did not prohibit what pertains to divine praise and worship.

Now and then, the commands of the law seem unbearably heavy. If our human nature does not point this out to us, there is an angelic nature always ready to whisper it to us; for our fight for perfection is not only against our own nature, but against the princes, the powers, the dominations of the angelic host who lost their own battle long ago. The abstract assurance of divine help against these vastly superior forces is a grand comfort; in the actual heat of the battle, it is a more solidly comforting thing to our human hearts to have before our eyes the concrete story of divinity's own strategies against Satanic cunning.

The temptation of Christ was just another of the devil's bad mistakes. He had to guess; and he guessed wrong. Not even an angelic intelligence could pierce through to the divinity of Christ, for that is something to be believed, not seen; the devil could see the sinless life of Christ and suspect the mystery, then remember the infant helplessness of Christ and doubt that God could make Himself so lowly. He could not believe, for belief flows only from a good will. Up to the last minutes of Christ's life, then, the devil was on tenterhooks about this strange Man; was He really God, or was He merely man?

It was fortunate for us that he made the mistake of trying to find the answer to that question. At least, his mistake protects us from foolish pride or smug security in our own sanctity. For sanctity is no guarantee against temptation; it is an invitation to it. The devil hates saints, they approach so closely to God; and, with the stupid stubbornness that has marked all of his career, he continues to batter his head against the divinely protected wall again and again. Really, sanctity and good works constitute a kind of diabolic desert where there is neither shade nor rest for the evil one. Indeed, sanctity is a desert place in another sense, for the corridors of sanctity are seldom crowded and man always faces his greatest dangers alone; so it was that Christ underwent His temptation when He was alone in a desert place. It was His invariable custom to face first the hardest of the things He demanded from us.

He went at that difficult task in a fashion that leaves no doubt in our minds as to the method we must pursue. There is no better preparation for future temptations than present fasting and penance. We know very well that there is no time in our lives when we can depend upon quiet security, rest on our arms idly waiting for the next fight to come up; surely we cannot take any chances on the grounds that we have worn down our strength with laborious good works. It was to a tired and hungry Christ, tired and hungry from fasting and penance, that the devil came. Whatever the cause of the fatigue, it is just at that time, with our body protesting a bit, that the devil is most likely to make his attack; he was never one to overlook so powerful an ally as our sense appetite.

His diabolic strategy in the temptation of Our Lord is worth noting well. Since temptation must always come from the outside as far as our soul is concerned, it must be by way of a suggestion. Being what we are, suggestion has no chance for infiltration except along a path already made smooth for the journeys of our heart. The devil does not shock a saint into alertness by suggesting great crimes; he starts off with little, almost inoffensive things to which even the heart of a saint would make only a mild protest. So it was with the temptation of Adam; so also with the temptation of Christ. These two heads of the race could not be grossly attacked; they were to be subtly fooled. To our first parents, the devil made an intellectual appeal, a suggestion to that element of curiosity in all of us, asking: "Why did God forbid this particular fruit?" With that wedge securely in, he became bolder, appealing to pride and vainglory with a promise that their eyes would be opened; it was only when definite progress seemed to have been made that the full horror of the temptation was made plain in his invitation to the extreme pride of rebellion—they should become like gods.

When the devil approached Christ, he used practically the same strategy—there is, after all, very little room for originality in the line of sin and temptation; he was perhaps a little more subtle with Christ, paying Him the same dubious compliment a bandit pays his victim in approaching him with extreme caution. He tempted Christ first with what even the most spiritual of men desire, the food necessary to sustain the body: "If thou be the Son of God, command that these stones be made bread." From there, he went on to that to which even spiritual men are too often victim, ostentation and vainglory: "If thou be the Son of God, cast thyself down..." (from the temple). With inevitable grossness, he advanced a temptation that appealed not to spiritual but to carnal men, the appeal of the riches and the glory of the world, going even so far as contempt of God: "All these will I give thee, if falling down thou wilt adore me."

The first thrust was not successful. Wisdom in the tempter would seem to indicate a complete change of attack, a search for some even subtler approach. But the devil is not wise, which is one of the reasons why he is a devil; the planned attack had to go forward, in spite of the failure of the first necessary maneuver, stupidly becoming clumsier at every step. It is no sin to trust in God, quite the contrary; but to plunge off a great height in deliberate temptation of God, demanding a miraculous rescue, that is a different matter. To desire riches and the honors of the world is not necessarily wrong; but to be willing to abandon God and adore the devil to attain those ends, there is no excuse for that. Christ was quite patient with the first two temptations, for, after all, He had come to conquer the devil by justice not by overwhelming divine power; at the third temptation, He lost all patience. He did more than reject the temptation, He dismissed the devil with a brusqueness that must have been gall to so proud a spirit. This temptation was not to be tolerated for an instant; for it was a direct attack, not on the things of men, but on God Himself.

That outburst of divine indignation sent the devil slinking away, still mystified by the God-man. When he had gone the angels came and ministered to their Master. We shall read once more of an angel ministering to a tired Christ; then it will be on the edge of His passion, as here He was on the threshold of His public life. Each was a beginning; and it is at just these moments that comfort is needed, for beginnings, particularly beginnings of divine things, are hard. Since then, it is not an angel but the Master Himself who brings comfort to the hearts of men courageous enough to begin.

From the desert, Christ returned to the cities of men and set off on His career of bearer of divine truth to men. Much later, this part of His life would be summed up with a simplicity whose beauty forbids adornment: He had done all things well. He spoke with the appeal and persuasiveness of an orator reading the hearts of his audience as plainly as the page of an open book; He denounced evil with the thundering authority of a supreme legislator; He confirmed His doctrine by stunning miracles, even more by the calm, persistent, quiet sinlessness of His life. All this was but the vehicle of His message. The doctrine itself surpassed anything that teachers of men have ever conceived; and it answered the deepest demands of the hearts and minds of men.

Yet, looked at objectively, the actual proposal of this doctrine seems to have been miserably limited. It was strictly held within the narrow limits of Palestine and, even there, was restricted to Christ's own people, the Jews. Why did not Our Lord preach to all men? How could He expect the same results from the lesser teachers to whom He commissioned this world-wide preaching? The point is that the lesser teachers actually achieved greater results, thereby showing more plainly the power behind that teaching.

Christ's restriction of His preaching to the chosen people was part of that orderly procedure so perfectly proper to God's action. The promises of a redeemer and a messiah had been made to the Jews, not to the Gentiles; the Jews, then, should receive the fulfillment of these promises. They were the chosen people, they had had generations of preparation; they should be given the first chance to welcome the Messiah....

He came to the Jews in fulfillment of divine promises, in the name of God's love of the race. His love was the strong love of God, a love great enough to be terribly severe. By their malice, the leaders of this chosen people were impeding the salvation of the whole race; they were rejecting the doctrine of Christ which alone held out hope of salvation; their vices were corrupting the life of the people. This was not the time for a lover of the people and a teacher of truth to tread gently lest he hurt the feelings of some who were considered great among men. Of course Christ cried out against them, sparing them nothing; yet there was the full vigor of divine love in that violence, a love that embraced the leaders perhaps even more strongly than the people who followed them....

When in the last days of His life, Christ was called to account, He could say with complete truth "I have spoken nothing in secret." He had not come to hide divine truth but to manifest it; He was not a miserly Master huddling over His knowledge in dark corners, gloating over His exclusive possession of it, afraid to share it lest He lose His mastery. The things He had to say needed nothing of the garments of sly ambiguity which hide the ugliness of the obscene and allow it to slip furtively into the souls of men. Christ taught publicly: to crowds in the temple, on the sea shore, in desert places, on the high road. To the little group of apostles and disciples, He talked incessantly. He let slip no opportunity to publish His truth. Some things He spoke to the multitudes in parables, giving them the milk of children because they were not capable of the meat of men; clearly, it was better for them to have this than nothing at all. Even these parables were explained in detail to the apostles to whom it was given to know the secrets of the kingdom of God that they might instruct the children of men.

Many years after, closing his own attempt to put the teachings and deeds of Christ in the prison of written words, St. John admitted the hopelessness of it: "There are also many other things which Jesus did, which if they were written every one, the world itself, I think, would not be able to contain the books that should be written." The world could not contain the books, only heaven can; it is quite impossible to contain the sublimity of the teachings of divine wisdom within the narrow confines of words. Christ Himself wrote no words beyond those few He scrawled in the sand to scatter the accusers of the adulteress; how significant that it should have been sand in which He wrote! He did His real writing on the hearts of men and thus forever scotched the petty error that His doctrine was not more than is contained in the written Scriptures....

While the written word did not befit the dignity of Christ, His miracles certainly did. There was nothing confining about them; rather, they threw open the vast spaces of infinity to the human mind. Indeed, their whole service is to lift the mind of a man above the limits of nature by bringing him into sharp contact with the Author of nature. A miracle is a wave of divine power that lifts men up to the crest and lets them see the distant shore if only for an instant. More concretely, they are worked either to confirm the truth or to show the presence of God in the man who does the works of God. On both counts, Christ fittingly worked miracles.

The miracles of Christ, like all true miracles, were worked by divine power, for miracles are such precisely because they outstrip the powers of nature. It is true that Christ reached out and touched the leper to cleanse him, it was His human voice that awoke Lazarus, Magdalen knew from His loving glance long before He spoke that her sins were forgiven; but the hand, the voice, the eye were merely instruments of divinity, channels which carried the power of God. Christ, even as an Infant in the manger, had both the divine power and the human instrumentality of that power, for He was both God and Man. It is, however, an extravagance of unbridled imagination to picture the childhood and adolescence of Christ as a gloriously triumphant journey leaving an uninterrupted wake of miracles behind it. If there was bread in the house at Nazareth, it was because it had been earned by Joseph and his Son: if the clothes were clean, it was because Mary had washed them.

There was no point in miracles until some truth was to be confirmed; until it was time to manifest the divinity of Christ to all men. The first miracle, then, is that recorded as such by St. John, the changing of water into wine at the marriage feast of Cana. It is comforting to remember that this first miracle was worked at Our Mother's request, that it was for such a human end as saving the host of Christ from embarrassment, that it was a benediction of such a human thing as marriage. I have often wondered what the bridegroom said to the master of the feast in answer to his complaint about saving the better wine until the last. Probably he just smiled and shrugged his shoulders, hoping Christ would not give him away.

From this beginning to the very end, all the miracles of Christ had the common purpose of confirming the truth of divinity, of manifesting to men the presence of God among them. All were, of course, works transcending natural powers; all were done in Christ's own name. Again and again, He insisted that it was in confirmation of His claim to divinity that He worked miracles; if what He said were not true, then God Himself would have collaborated in a gigantic lie.

Certainly, the scope of the miracles of Christ was a plainly written documentation of His mastery over all the universe, that is, of His divinity. Angelic beings bowed to His command in every expulsion of the demons from their possessed victims; the heavenly bodies offered their homage and submission when they covered their lace against the spectacle of the death of God. Most constantly, however, His miracles revolved around His fellow-men; of these, the outstanding ones are the healing miracles, the miracles whose final goal was not the salvation of the body but the soul. After all, He had come to save men, to enlighten their minds, and relieve them of the burden of sin. That no least doubt of His divinity might remain in the minds of men of good will, all irrational creation gave Him unquestioning obedience.

These were proud days in the lives of the apostles. The simple fishermen of Galilee were living familiarly with the Lord of the universe. Before their eyes, Nature tumbled over itself in its eagerness to obey Him; the eyes of faith showed them the greater miracles of grace within the souls of men; they shared His confidence, listened to His patient reiteration of divine truth, even partook of something of His infinite power on that mission where they were told to heal the sick, raise the dead, give freely of what they had freely received.

They returned from that journey bubbling over with enthusiasm, swelled a little with consciousness of self, to be met with the laconic word of the Master: "Let us go apart and rest a while." That is, let us stop for a minute to think, to remember, to pray; after all, you are the same men you were before, not God. As the days of His life grew shorter, His warnings of His passion and death grew more plain; to the apostles, they were steadily unwelcome, even a little frightening, shaking that confidence and sense of power that had so recently come to them.

They had some reason for fright. He was starting them off on a long journey over a road that was rough and steep. His divine wisdom could easily understand that the comforting memories of three intimate years with Him would hardly be enough for them. In the kindness of His heart, He gave them concrete, ocular evidence of some of the joys that awaited them at the end of the journey. For an instant, there on Tabor, Christ unveiled to His beloved three the glory of His human soul shining through His human body.

Understand, this transfiguration was a revelation of human glory. It was essentially the same brilliance that is a permanent quality of the bodies of the saints after the resurrection, the brilliance that would have been constantly shining forth from the body of Christ had not a constant miracle been worked to prevent what would have overwhelmed men as it did the apostles on Tabor. This glimpse of glory completed the dim sketch of the glory of the human body after the resurrection. Other vague details had been drawn when Christ passed through the closed womb of the Virgin, when He walked upon the water, when He passed unharmed through the hands of the Jews who attempted to apprehend Him before His hour had come.

This apex of human glory was not only for the men who were to come after Christ, but for those faithful ones who had preceded Him. Fittingly, then, Moses and Elijah were present at that preview of glory in the name of all who had gone before; Peter, James and John, in the name of all who were to come after. Those five witnesses were really a mighty company; the Law and the Prophets, the Head of the Church, the first of the apostolic martyrs, the most beloved of the disciples and greatest of the evangelists, the Sons of Thunder, and the Rock upon which Christ was to build His Church.

The transfiguration of Christ was really a revelation of the full significance of our position as adopted sons of God. By that adoption, we are made conformable to the natural Son of God, imperfectly now by grace with its glory for the soul, perfectly in heaven with its glory for the body and soul. We enter the life of grace by baptism, the life of heaven by the light of glory. As at the baptism of Christ, so here again at His transfiguration, there is the divine witness to His natural Sonship and a divine promise as to our adopted sonship. As at the baptism the Son was baptized and the Holy Ghost appeared hovering over Him in the form of a dove, while the Father's voice was heard approving; so here on Tabor, the Son was glorified, the Father testified, and the Holy Ghost hovered over the scene in a luminous cloud.

They came down from the mountain a little shaken to set about the business of suffering and dying. But now, what a different task it was, not only for them but for all men; for here was the goal that explained all the hardships and difficulties of the journey—the vision of glory within a man now, shining through His very body in heaven. Here was the secret of the glory of man: a human sharing in the divine life.

CARYLL HOUSELANDER

PHILIP SPEAKS

When we returned and told Him all we had done,
I, for one, was emptied out like a husk
that has scattered its seed upon hard ground.

We had not had time even to eat;
always the open hand,
always the blind eyes,
always the deaf ears,
always the wound to be healed.

My thoughts were like wild birds
beating the bars of the cage
for empty skies.

Even now the smell of the people
clung to my hair and clothes.

A rotten sweetness of oil and musk
that smells like death, it hung in my hair.

Their voices went on and on in my head,
monotonous waves wearing my mind away.
(Rock is worn by the waves to sand.)
I wanted to shut my mind, that my thoughts might close
on my own peace; I wanted to close
the peace of my love in my heart,
like dew in a dark rose.

He told us to rest.

We went in a small ship,
the wind and water moving in her.
She lived in their sweetness of life, a bride.
Her sail, a white wing—unmoving—moved with the tide.
She lay to the wind, and we gave our hearts with a sigh
to the breath of the Spirit of love.

But when we came to the shore
the people were there;
they had found us out:
always the open hand,
always the blind eyes,
always the deaf ears,

always the wounds to be healed!
They were there,
swarming there, everywhere—
insects there in the sun
when someone has lifted a stone.
I knew they would drain Him
and wring Him out—wring Him out
to the last drop of the fountain-water of Life
I was sick of it all,
with a dry husk for a heart.

But He saw the flocks wanting shepherd and fold;
pity in Him rose in a clear spring
for the world's thirst, and love was a pastureland.

So it went on all day:
always the open hand,
always the dull mind,
always the slow heart,
always the nameless fears;
and self-pity, sell-pity and tears;

until the sun went up in the blaze of the day's heat,
and with red wine burning through thin gold,
it was lowered slowly onto the altar-stone
of the darkening world, where the sheep were in fold.

We thought, "Now it is night; He will send them away;
the hour is late." We said, "This is a desert place.
Send them away, Lord, to buy food and be fed!"
But He: "You give them to eat!"

The grass in that place shone exceedingly green.
I remember, because when the brain is dust
the cool greenness of grass is absurdly sweet.

"There is a lad here," said Andrew,
"with two little fish and five loaves of bread.
But what are these, if this crowd must be fed?"
"Bid them sit down on the grass, and give them to eat,"
the Lord said.

The lad was one of the crowd; he went as he came.
As long as the world lasts, the world will remember him,
but no one will know his name!

They sat down on the grass.
My heart contracted, my mind was withered up;
but Christ poured out His tenderness,
like wine poured out into a lifted cup.

Always the open hands,
always the blind eyes,

always the mouth to be fed;
and I, for one, was emptied out like a husk
that has scattered its seed upon hard ground.
But He saw the flocks wanting shepherd and fold;
pity in Him rose in a clear spring
for the world's thirst, and love was a pastureland.

The Lord blessed the bread.
He put it into our hands and it multiplied,
not in His hands but in mine!

Even now, remembering this,
my thoughts shut like a folding wing;
my mind is a blank sheet of light in the mystery of
the thing.
I gave and my hands were full, again and again;
pity in Him fell on my dry dust:
it was summer rain,
and the husk of my heart expanded and filled again
and was large with grain.

For me, the miracle was this:
that a clear stream of the Lord's love—
not mine—
flowed out of my soul,
a shining wave over my fellow men.

These things I have told you happened a long while since.
Our cherished Lord is dead; He was crucified.
Now, as then, we go about in the crowd, telling His love
and how He rose from the dead and, risen in us,
He lives in the least of men.
But I think nobody understands,
until I touch their wounds and they know
the healing of His hands.

On the night of the Pasch, before He died,
He blessed the bread and put it into my hands,
to increase and be multiplied to the end of time.

Now, if I turned my face from the market-place,
I should be haunted, hearing the rustle of wheat in
the darkness—
striving, pushing up to the light.
I should hear His words, falling like slow tears
in the upper-room,
when He prayed that we all be one,
even as they are one, the Father and Son:

falling like slow tears
over the sown fields;
and I should see the world
like a young field of wheat

growing up for the grain,
watered by Christ's tears.

Always the open hands,
always the blind eyes,
always the slow mind,
always the deaf ears,
and always Christ, Our Lord,
crowned with the flowering thorn
and ringed with spears.

I know—now that I never see
the print of His feet in the dust
where the Son of Man trod—
that in every man, forever,
I meet the Son of God.

THE BOOK OF THE SAVIOUR ❧ VOLUME TWO

KARL ADAM

❧ ❧

PERFECT MAN

The powerful impression which Jesus made at sight on ordinary people and especially on the sick and on sinners certainly owed something to his appearance, which drew all to him and held them, even if it was primarily due to his spiritual and religious power. His eyes with their burning, wakening, reproving looks must have been especially striking. Does not he himself say "the light of thy body is the eye. If thy eye be single, thy whole body shall be lightsome"? It is significant that Mark, when reporting some important saying of Our Lord, not seldom uses some such expression as "And looking round about on them he saith."

Coupled with this exterior comeliness we get the impression of health, power, energy and well-being in the appearance of Jesus. According to the unanimous witness of the Gospels Jesus must have been a thoroughly healthy man, inured to fatigue and with a great capacity for work. In this he is differentiated from other important founders of religions. Muhammed was a sickly man, tainted with an hereditary disease and with a shattered nervous system, when he unfolded the banner of the prophet. Buddha was mentally a broken-down and worn-out man when he died. We never hear of Jesus that he was visited by any sickness. All the sufferings which came to him were due to his calling, to the privations and sacrifices which his messianic mission laid on him. His body must have been hardened in no common measure. A proof of this is seen in his habit of beginning his work in the early morning. "Rising very early, going out he went into a desert place and there he prayed" (Mark 1:35); "When day was come, he called unto him his disciples: and he chose twelve of them" (Luke 4:13); his joy in nature breathes the same fresh, healthy, unspent sensibility. The hills and the lake were especially dear to him. After a tiring day's work he loved to climb to some lonely height or late in the evening get himself taken on to the shimmering water of the Lake of Genesareth and stay out far into the night. We know further that the whole of his public life was one of wandering, coming and going from Galilee to Samaria and Judaea and even as far as to the district of Tyre and Sidon. And he made these journeys with the simplest provision for the way, as he would also have his disciples do. "Take nothing for your journey, neither staff, nor scrip, nor bread, nor money, neither have two coats" (Luke 9:3). Hunger and thirst must therefore often have accompanied him. His last journey from Jericho up to Jerusalem is rightly pointed to as an astounding feat. Under a burning sun, along roads in which there was no shade of any kind, through a desolate rocky waste he had to mount some three thousand five hundred feet in his six hours' climb. And the most astonishing thing is that Jesus was not tired. On the very same evening he took part in a feast which Lazarus and his sisters had made ready for him. By far the greatest part of his public ministry was spent not in the comfort of a home, but in the open, exposed to all the rigours of the climate.

He was born and died in remote places. Between the manger of Bethlehem and the hill of Golgotha he spent a life more homeless and poor than that of the birds in their nests and the foxes in their holes. If he ever entered a house, it was one belonging to acquaintances or friends. For himself he had not where to lay his head. There can be no doubt that Jesus must have spent the night in the open many hundreds of times and that it was not least this that made the birds of the air and the lilies of the field so familiar to him. Only an absolutely sound body could have been equal to such demands on it. Moreover, this wandering life was filled to overflowing with labour and toil. Again and again Mark notes the fact that they had not time to eat (cf. Mark 3:20; 6:31). Till late in the evening the sick kept coming and going. And with the sick there came malevolent enemies, the Pharisees and Sadducees, and word wrestled with word, mind with mind, and racking disputes took place, leading to dangerous moments of tension and conflict.

In addition there were the tiring explanations he had to make to his own disciples and the heavy burden which their want of understanding and their self-seeking laid upon him. Any sickly or even weak constitution must have given in or broken down under the strain. That Jesus never on any occasion gave in, not even in the most tense or dangerous situations, that, for instance, in the midst of a raging storm on the Lake of Genesareth he went on peacefully sleeping until his disciples woke him, and that suddenly roused from his deep sleep he immediately grasped the situation and dealt with it, all this is proof how far his nature was from being excitable and temperamental, what complete control he had over his senses, how sound he was in body.

Was there also a sound mind in this sound body?... The first to slander him by saying "he is become mad" were his own relations (Mark 3:21). And his adversaries among the Pharisees only put the same thing in their own way when they assumed that an evil spirit was working in him (Matt. 12:24).

The evangelists give us unequivocal information on this point. What struck them most in his human nature and what they were always underlining was the tremendous clarity of his thought, the sure consciousness he had of his aim, and the resultant inflexibility and finality of his will. If one wished to attempt the impossible and to sum up his mentality in one phrase, he would have to set down this resolute virility and fixity of purpose with which Jesus sees his Father's will as his appointed task, and carries it through to the very end, even to the pouring out of his own blood. His very turn of phrase, with its ever-recurring "I am come," "I am not come," gives expression to the stern determined Yea and Nay of his life and the inflexibility of his purpose. "I came not to send peace, but a sword"; "I am not come to call the just, but sinners"; "The Son of Man is come to seek and to save that which was lost"; "The Son of Man is not come to be ministered to, but to minister, and to give his life a ransom for many"; "Do not think I am come to destroy the law or the prophets. I am not come to destroy, but to fulfil"; "I am come to cast fire on the earth; and what will I but that it be kindled?" Jesus knows what he wills and he knew it from the beginning. In the scene in the temple at Jerusalem when he was but a twelve-year-old lad, he gave clear and plain expression to what his life's work was to be. "Did you not know that I must be about my Father's business?"

The temptations in the desert are, psychologically regarded, a victorious settlement with the Satanic possibility of using his own messianic powers for his own self-glorification and selfish ends and not for the construction of the Kingdom of God. We can see here with the utmost clearness how plainly, at the very start of his ministry, Jesus sees the new way, and how resolutely he treads it, the way of self-surrender and of sacrifice for the heavenly Father's sake. In the days that followed it was not only his enemies who sought to divert him from it. On at least three occasions we can trace influences from within his own circle at work to force him to abandon the *via dolorosa* on which he had set out. At Capharnaum these are already vaguely in evidence in the secret opposition of his own kindred. They came to a head in Peter's determined protest at Caesarea Philippi: "Lord, be it far from thee, this shall not be unto thee." And they led once, when Jesus spoke of the eating of his flesh and the drinking of his blood (John 6:57), to a mass-defection of his own followers. "After this many of his disciples went back; and walked no more with him." But Jesus pursued his way, determined, if need be, to follow it alone and solitary. He has no reassuring words on this occasion for his disciples. He only puts to them the short, sharp question, "Will you also go away?" Here we have Jesus, the man of clear will, whose every action reveals the fixity of his purpose. In the whole of his public ministry not one single instant can be found when he had to reflect on an answer or when he hesitated in indecision or when he reversed a statement or an action. And he demands the same inflexible and steadfast purpose of his disciples. "No man, putting his hand to the plough, and turning back, is fit for the Kingdom of God"; "Which of you having a mind to build a tower, doth not first sit down and reckon the charges that are necessary?" or "What king minded to make war does not first make a muster of his troops?" It is his own method quite personal to himself that he here enjoins on his disciples.

Unconsidered action, vacillation, any coming to terms or compromising, these are not for him. His whole life and being are a Yea and Nay, nothing else. Jesus is always the complete man, always prepared, for he never speaks or acts except out of his whole clear consciousness and his own firm will. Hence he and he alone can venture the imperative "Let your speech be yea, yea: no, no: and that which is over and above these is evil" (Matt. 5:37). His whole nature and life are a unity, a completeness, a transparency, are fundamental clarity and truth. He bore so clearly the marks of the true, the upright, and the strong, that even his enemies could not escape this impression. "Master, we know that thou art a true speaker and carest not for any man." Here, in the unity and purity and transparency of his interior life, lies the psychological point whence started his life's struggle against the Pharisees, those "whited sepulchres," representative of the spurious, the finical, the purely exterior and the narrow in religion and life. From this point his way led directly to the Cross. It was, psychologically speaking, his tragic fate that he throughout remained true to himself, to that genuineness and loyalty to himself and his Father's will which was his nature.

Jesus is in every respect an heroic, epic figure, heroism incarnate. And it was this heroic spirit, this unconditional staking of their lives for the known truth, that he demanded also of his disciples. The heroic is to him a matter of course. To the rich young man who had observed all the commandments but one thing was wanting, that he should sell all he had and follow Jesus. The true disciple must be so valiant, so resolutely purposeful, that he will not even take the time to bury his own father. "Let the dead bury their dead." His concern must not be for the dead but for the living. What makes a disciple a disciple is that he "hate his father and mother and children and brethren and sisters, yea and his own life also"; that is to say, in the Aramaic figure of speech, that he set all these aside in order to follow Jesus.

This concentration and focussing of the will on his goal, this initiative and energy, make Jesus the born leader. He called Simon and Andrew, "and immediately leaving their nets they followed him." He called James and John "and leaving their father Zebedee in the ship with his hired men, they followed him." He cast out them that bought and sold in the temple and none ventured to resist him. His is a masterful nature, a regal disposition.

The disciples felt this. Hence their diffident awe of the Master, their strong sense of the gulf separating them from him, which kept them at a distance. Again and again the evangelists note how they wondered among themselves at his words or actions, how these struck terror into them (Mark 9:5; 6:51; 4:40; 10:24, 26), and how they did not dare speak to him (Mark 9:31). Mark describes the start of the last journey to Jerusalem with the significant words: "And Jesus went before them, and they were astonished, and following were afraid."

This same timidity and awe also affected the multitude. "And they were afraid," "and all men wondered." He was not like one of them, neither was he like one of their own leaders, the scribes and Pharisees. He was one having authority. So strong was the impression of towering ascendency in the figure of Jesus that the people sought the loftiest images and names to find words to express it. Is he John the Baptist? Is he Elijah? Is he Jeremiah, or one of the prophets? Jesus was fully conscious of the essential difference between himself and all other men. Hence he loved solitude. So soon as he had spent himself in preaching to and healing the multitude, he withdrew into himself and betook himself to some lonely spot or on to some silent hill. Again and again this is noted by the evangelist. "And having dismissed the multitude, he went into a mountain alone to pray." It was a solitude *in sinu patris,* that is to say, a solitude shared with the Father. But it was nevertheless a withdrawal from the multitude into himself, a silence of his concentrated forces, a silence whence as from some hidden well the living water gushed forth.

It was a psychological necessity that this tremendously concentrated and disciplined will, this pent-up spiritual power, should discharge itself in stern language and bold action when powers of evil arrayed themselves against him. On such occasions Jesus could wax wroth and show his displeasure like any prophet of the Old Testament, an Hosea or a Jeremiah, or like Moses when he threw the tables of the law to the ground. This must be recognized, if we would get to know Jesus. In Jesus there dwelt not only mighty powers held in restraint and a disciplined will, but the fire of a holy zeal. We need only test his words and actions for their emotional content to verify this. "Begone, Satan," was how he frightened away the devil who came to tempt him. "Go behind me, Satan, thou art a scandal unto me," was how he rebuked Peter when the latter wished to break down his will to pursue the road which led to the Cross. "I know you not, whence you are: depart from me, you that work iniquity," is what he will profess to those who have neglected to do good to his suffering brethren on earth. It is not quiet, peaceful reserve of spirit that we have here, but deep emotion and passion. Not a few of his parables breathe the same fiery spirit. In them the thunder rolls and the lightning flashes, as in the parable of the cockle: "The Son of Man shall send his angels, and they shall gather out of his kingdom all scandals and them that work iniquity. And shall cast them into the furnace of fire. There shall be weeping and gnashing of teeth." Similarly, too, in the parable of the fishermen's net: "The angels shall go out and shall separate the wicked from among the just. And shall cast them into the furnace of fire: there shall be weeping and gnashing of teeth." The same angry sentence is also pronounced in the parables of the ten virgins, the talents and the sheep and the goats. In the parable of the unmerciful servant the king "being angry delivered him to the torturers until he paid all the debt." Again, in the parable of the marriage of the king's son, the king "was angry, and sending his armies, he destroyed those murderers and burned their city."

And when later on the king saw a man at the feast who had not on a wedding garment, he in unconcealed anger gave the order: "Bind his hands and feet, and cast him into the exterior darkness: there shall be weeping and gnashing of teeth." And in his similitude of the faithful and unfaithful stewards, the lord of the house returns unexpectedly and orders the latter to be beaten with many stripes, and "appoints him his portion with the unbelievers."

There can be no doubt but that the temperament which gave birth to these parables was charged full with emotion. Of sentimentality there is not a trace. As for the polemics against the scribes and the Pharisees, against the ruling caste, against the teachers of Israel, and the judgments passed on them, they flame with indignation. "Woe to you scribes and Pharisees, hypocrites; because you devour the houses of widows, praying long prayers. For this you shall receive the greater judgment ... You blind guides, who strain at a gnat and swallow a camel.... Woe to you scribes and Pharisees, hypocrites: because you make clean the outside of the cup and of the dish: but within you are full of rapine and uncleanness" (Matt. 23:14, 24, 25). The same temperamental vehemence and heat breaks out in not a few of his actions, especially in the cleansing of the temple when "he cast out them that sold and bought in the temple, and overthrew the tables of the money-changers and the chairs of them that sold doves. And he suffered not that any man should carry a vessel through the temple" (Mark 11:15ff.). And it is also displayed in the malediction of the fig-tree on which there was not yet fruit, "for it was not the time for figs." In both these cases his wrath took a form likely to alienate those who regarded these events by themselves. The merchants in the court of the temple thought that they were acting fully within their rights; for they had, with the knowledge and consent of the Jewish authorities, leased their trading rights from Annas. Then again the fig-tree was quite blameless in not having any fruit in early spring. But it was distinctive of the prophetic, and particularly of the Messianic method, to announce by apparent paradoxes, and by unintelligible acts, the new unprecedented, revolutionary character of the Messianic message. The very paradox of his actions will necessarily call attention to the prophet and his revolutionary influence. Hence the evangelists have a special interest in the cleansing of the temple, and each of them gives an account of it (Matt. 21:12ff.; Mark 11:15ff.; Luke 19:45ff.; John 2:14ff.); and in telling the curse put upon the fig-tree Mark is careful to add the words, "for it was not the time for figs" (11:13). It is in the unusual that the Messiah is manifest to them. In the seemingly unfair and inconsiderate casting out of the merchants from the temple, they see the solemn proclamation of the newly arisen Messianic worship of God in spirit and in truth, of the new Messianic temple and of the destruction of the old, a proclamation destructive of all merely earthly ambitions. The apparently senseless curse put upon the fig-tree is, to their minds, precisely because of its harsh unintelligibility, a prophetical symbol of the approaching sinister curse on Israel, that fig-tree which the Lord had himself planted, and which had remained unfruitful in good seasons as well as bad. There is hardly another place in the Gospels where the Messianic background, against which the life of Jesus as related in them is enacted, is more evident. Whosoever does not see this background can only misunderstand Jesus.

Jesus was not one to tread delicately, he was no timid weakling when the need arose to bear witness to the truth. His was a fighter's nature. But here, too, in the midst of the fight, he always remains himself, he never forgets himself, never loses control. His anger is always an expression of supreme moral freedom, the act of one having full knowledge, of one who could say, "for this came I into the world, that I should give testimony to the truth." It is because he was so consistently true to his Father's will, because he was only "Yea and Nay" that he reacted with equal severity against anything that was ungodly or hateful to God, whether this found expression in perverse theological formularies or in the decree of a ruler. And the story of his life proves that in harmony with his uncompromising words he was ready to stake his own life for the truth and to die for it.

C. C. MARTINDALE, S.J.

TRUE SON OF ABRAHAM

Our Lord had the normal experiences to which human flesh is heir—hunger, thirst, fatigue, responsiveness to all that can challenge the senses. That He was hungry, we know. In days when earning had ceased, but publicity and, in consequence, alms had not been obtained and made normal, He and His companions were driven to plucking the ears of wheat as they passed by the field's edge, and rubbing them between their hands so as to get the grain. He was tired, and at Sychar sent His disciples ahead into the city to buy food while He Himself sat down "thus" under the shade beside the ancient well, and asked a local woman to give him something to drink.... True, in the eagerness of the apostolate which forthwith became possible, He asked no more for the cool water and could not bring Himself to want to eat what the disciples carried back; but the fact remained, true hunger and true thirst had been there first. He was so tired on that occasion when they crossed the lake, that He could not take His place at the oar, but went to sleep "with His head upon a cushion." I must confess to you that after that first crowded day at Capharnaum, when at last the thrilled crowds had left Him and then very early next day returned to make the most of Him once more, and found Him not, for He had "risen up, very early, while it was still dark, and gone out into a lonely place to pray"—all this touches me, yet perhaps not so suddenly or poignantly as the recollection that between whiles, our Lord, the Saviour of the world, had been lying asleep, on mat, beneath rug, head on bolster, fast asleep, in the little house of Peter. Is any one thing more human than to go to sleep?

But the days came when it was a danger to receive Him; when the little village would not, in fact, receive Him when He wished to enter it after the long dusty tramp, to find His meal; and even, when He would have to say, very gravely, though not bitterly, to one who professed a wish to follow Him, that the foxes had their holes and the flying birds their nests, but that as for Him, He had not where to lay His head. That was when, upon lime-stone rock and under tamarisk or juniper, our Lord found for the night such shelter as He could.

I am not going to pursue our Lord's human experiences beyond these bodily ones, into either those mental ones which are concerned with deep personal joys or sorrows; or into those emotional ones which are proper to the having, say, of friends. But you must let me just allude to one little explosion, as it were, of intense appreciation of beauty on His part which is so incidental that we seldom notice all that it implies. He is speaking of God's Providence, and how it prolongs itself into all parts of nature—animal nature—not one sparrow falls to the ground without God, who is its Father, knowing all about it and making it, somehow, *right*; and indeed, into inanimate nature. Owing to God and not to us, the flowers spring up and grow—it is not they who clothe themselves; they weave not neither do they spin... and then, suddenly, our Lord glances off, as it were, from this thought into a kind of ecstasy at their sheer beauty—indeed, He had the incentive: Palestine in spring is a mass of anemones, cyclamen, iris: blue, lilac, palest pink and crimson, yellow and cream and purple—but what an exclamation is, as it were, wrested from Him: "I tell you, not Solomon, in *all* his glory, was arrayed like *one* of these!" You might find in ancient literature some instances of the more or less convinced rehearsal of that classical cliché which declares that nature is more beautiful than art; but on the lips of a Jew, of one given indeed to admiring the force and even violence of nature, the richness of tilth and luxuriance of vine or forest, but perfectly imperceptive, you would think, of the more tender charm and of the delicacies of living things that were not human—this cry of ecstasy, I repeat, this sweeping elimination of Solomon, the very symbol of magnificence, is something completely new, something that entrances us with its humanity when we encounter it, and enough to make us gratefully rejoice in the *total* humanity of Him who was known as Joseph's son, and chose for His habitual title, "Son of Man."

He was also true son of Joseph, son of David, son of Abraham, because He *thought in the way proper to such a man.* We are all half consciously inclined to assume that the really right way of thinking is the one in which our fellow-countrymen think, and that other nationalities somehow deviate from it—inculpably, no doubt, and without being able to help it; but all the same, their thoughts are rather "queer" and the simpler sort of tourist undoubtedly feels that it is rather perverse of a Frenchman so much as to talk French, and as for Czech.... It remains that nations and races really have their *way* of thinking; and by that I do not mean that they entertain a perfectly different set of thoughts from ours, but that they think the same things in a different way, and clothe their ideas in correspondingly different words, and, above all, in a quite different costumery, so to say, supplied by an imagination immemorially furnished in a particular way. Now when Our Lord thought of Tyre and Sidon, when we might think of Brighton or Blackpool, Marseilles or Monte Carlo, Shanghai or Buenos Aires (or any two other towns which we find it more convenient to criticise than our own), He really did most naturally think of them. He was not playing a part, and, as it were, saying to Himself: "Tyre and Sidon are the sorts of places that these Palestinians require to have mentioned to them—I will introduce some local colour." When Solomon, the Queen of Sheba, this or that prophet, was alluded to by Him, it was not as though we, in Italy, might courteously choose to mention Dante or d'Annunzio rather than Shakespeare or Rupert Brooke. When He argued as He did with the Pharisees He adopted methods strange to us—not as an Englishman, laboriously or with that instinctive skill which makes the really useful civil servant overseas, might adapt his mind and his palaver to Swahili or Matabele; but He spoke like that because such really were the processes of His human mind—Jewish processes proper to that age, because he *was* a Jew, living exactly then.

Moreover, He loved that land of His with all His heart. He had, personally and so far as His actual life-time went, a very circumscribed mission. "I am not sent but to the lost sheep of the House of Israel." The pagan officer, whose boy He cured, the pagan woman to whom He said (seemingly so roughly) that it was not right to take the household bread and toss it to the dogs—and who (dare I say?) defeated Him so exquisitely by answering that anyway the little dogs beneath the table ate the crumbs that happened to fall from it—extorted His half exultant, half agonized admiration : "I have not yet found such faith—no, not in Israel itself!" But primarily, and genuinely, His efforts personally went to save "at least in this its day"—in the last few hours more for which that day was destined to last—His own People. Jerusalem was the centre of the spiritual life of any Jew; twice did our Lord cry His heart out when, from Mount Olivet, He saw the walls that so soon were to be laid low. But even so, Christ was, as we might say, a north-countryman; He came from Galilee; and no one can fail to "sense" the sorrow, the bitter, bitter grief, of His heart when for the last time He said goodbye to those hills and to the lake and took His way towards Jerusalem, where they would kill Him.

EILEEN DUGGAN

NATIONALITY

Because He was a man
As well as He was God,
He loved His own goat-nibbled hills,
His crumbling Jewish sod.
He bowed to Roman rule
And dared none to rebel
But Oh the windflowers out of Naim
We know He loved them well!
He must have loved its tongue,
His Aramaic brogue,
As much as any Norman loves
The accents of La Hogue.
Discountried and diskinged
And watched from pole to pole,
A Jew at heart remains a Jew—
His nation is his soul.

Had He upon that day
Of headlong cloaks and boughs
Surrendered all mankind to race
And lifted David's brows,
They would not on His cross
Have writ as mocking news
That He the man from Nazareth
Was monarch of the Jews.
As heifers' to their young
Christ's bowels yearned to His sod.
He was the very Jew of Jews
And yet since He was God—
Oh you with frontiered hearts,
Conceive it if you can—
It was not life alone
He gave, But country up for man.

RONALD KNOX

THE PATIENCE OF CHRIST

"Burning heat by day, and biting frost at nights, till my eyelids lost the power of sleep"—so Jacob describes his twenty long years of service under Laban. And the Son of Man had not where to lay his head; all day he taught the multitude; at evening he answered the questions propounded to him by his apostles; sometimes it was only by denying himself sleep altogether that he could find time for prayer. In all this, he would be a model for his priests; they were to be, all the time, at *everybody's* disposal, they were not to keep office hours. And whereas we are accustomed to remember how tired Our Lord must have been *physically* by the labours he undertook during the years of his active ministry, we are apt to forget how tired he must have been mentally. After all, his nerves, no less than his muscles, were ordinary human nerves, capable of exhaustion. Nothing is so fatiguing, I fancy, as the pressure of multitudinous other human lives on our own. How easily we priests recognize the types of people who surrounded Our Lord with their comments and their questionings! The unfriendly critic who wants a reason for everything: "How is it that thy disciples do not fast, when John's disciples and the Pharisees fast?" The eager inquirer who, after all, never comes up to the scratch: "Lord, give me leave to go home and bury my father first." The person who cannot understand what a priest's job is and what it is not: "Master, bid my brother give me a share of our inheritance." The pious female who pesters you with her compliments: "Blessed is the womb that bore thee..." and all the rest of them. Our Lord met them all, and always with a patient word. Day in, day out, they never left him alone.

OSCAR WILDE

E TENEBRIS

Come down, O Christ, and help me! reach Thy hand,
For I am drowning in a stormier sea
Than Simon on Thy Lake of Galilee:
The wine of life is spilled upon the sand.
My heart is as some famine-murdered land
Whence all good things have perished utterly,
And well I know my soul in Hell must lie
If I this night before God's throne should stand.

"He sleeps, perchance, or rideth to the chase,
Like Baal, when his prophets howled that name
From morn till noon on Carmel's smitten height."
Nay, peace I shall behold before the night,
The feet of brass, the robe more white than flame,
The wounded hands, the weary human face.

ALFRED NOYES

❧ ❧

NEVER MAN SPAKE

The historical Figure had disappeared. The foot-prints on the shore of Galilee had vanished. The miracles, if any had been wrought, could no longer be investigated. But something yet remained. There were certain recorded utterances which could be examined here and now. If the supreme claim of the Christian philosophy as to the nature of its Founder were true there should be something more than remarkable in the nature of those utterances; something that would reveal itself to the cold and impartial tests whereby we estimate the values of isolated passages in great literature; something in the very quality of those utterances (apart from all other considerations) that came up to the level of the supreme claim....

The mental process by which we recognize and appreciate the comparative values of isolated passages in great literature, or discover the author in his work, is not an analytical one. It differs from those of the textual critic and the theologian. But it is rational. There is a profound philosophy behind it; and its principles belong to the great history of aesthetics from Plato to Hegel. Whatever failings it may have in its adventures among contemporaries, it knows nothing of partisanship or prejudice among the masterpieces of the remote past. Its function there is a spiritual one, the recognition of spirit by spirit, through material forms, or the harmonies of language. It is in their qualities that it knows them, and it asks for no other corroboration....

Doubts and controversies may arise over inferior examples, where the artistic values are themselves obscured. But only those who do not know the exquisite precisions and certainties of the highest level of art would distrust their evidence in the noblest cases; and in actual fact it is by their evidence alone that the highest achievements of creative genius in art and literature hold their immortal place in the history of mankind. Höffding, dealing with the symbolic element in religious ideas, had taught that the religious consciousness approximates to the aesthetic point of view, and adopted the mental process of the latter as an essential part of his philosophy of religion. Kant, Hegel, Schiller, Wordsworth and many others, by many independent considerations, had already justified him. It was the mental process with which I was most familiar; and I was haunted by the feeling that it had something of the first importance to tell me about the utterances of the central Figure in the history of religion; and especially, to begin with, that quiet personal reassurance addressed to a mourner at a graveside: *I am the Resurrection and the Life.*

Through all the veils of translation, in Greek, Latin, or English, it seemed to convey values unlike any other that had fallen from human lips. If we compared the loftiest utterances of Socrates or Shakespeare with that sublimely simple statement of its Author's *personal* mastery over the entire kingdom of death, the distance between them was at once seen to be an infinite distance. This infinite distance required an adequate explanation from the literary critic no less than from the theologian. A difference beyond measure seemed, at first sight, to postulate a cause beyond measure.

Shakespeare, the accepted master of merely human speech, might by a considerable expenditure of rhetoric impress us with his power to write a poem that would "live."

> *"So long as men can breathe, or eyes can see,*
> *So long lives this, and this gives life to thee."*

But his words are gnats dancing in the sun compared with the stupendous implications of that quiet reassurance, addressed to a woman mourning for the dead, and not only to her, but to all those who have ever looked down speechlessly into a grave— *I am the Resurrection and the Life.*

I am not here discussing the truth of that quiet reassurance, all the more heart-shaking for its profound and infinite calm, nor am I resuscitating the familiar and powerful, but not wholly convincing argument, "either a madman or God." I am looking at the problem for the moment from the point of view of pure literature, and the values whereby we estimate its greatness, those strange values of the eternal world which, in certain inspired moments, seem to emerge from the almost miraculously perfect arrangement of a few colours on a canvas, a few recorded words from the lips of Socrates, a few lines on a printed page, or a combination of three sounds in music, from which there emerges "not a fourth sound, but a star."

"The Divine," said Hegel, "is the centre of all the representations of art." In the highest moments of art and literature, our temporal world has always been seen *sub specie aeternitatis.* At such moments the masters of human expression have felt within themselves a spark of the divine Name, and acquired as Hartmann said, in his *Philosophy of the Unconscious,* the will and power to think and feel as if God were in them. At such times they seem to reveal fragments of the secret plan of the universe. They overhear phrases of the universal harmony and record them for men. But, however far these human masters may have risen above themselves in that process or have felt themselves inspired by a power greater than their own, there is not a measurable, but an utterly immeasurable distance between their utterance, and those quiet, superhuman, *personal* reassurances: *Let not your heart be troubled. Neither let it be afraid. Ye believe in God. Believe also in Me.... Come unto Me, all ye that are weary and heavy-laden, and ye shall find rest to your souls.*

There is egotism enough in literature, God knows; but what merely human being has been able to round the whole infinite circle from the supreme proclamation of Self as God's equal to the utter humility of a Self prepared to wash the dust of the wayside from the feet of one who would sell him for thirty pieces of silver.

Hereafter ye shall see the Son of Man coming in the clouds of heaven.... Take my yoke upon you and learn of Me; for I am meek and lowly of heart.

Were there ever such evidences of lowliness offered to God or man before? Could such evidences be offered—had the words any meaning at all if they came from a merely human being. How was it possible for any finite mind to ascend and descend thus in a single breath between earth and heaven—to claim the full majesty of the Eternal at one moment, and brood like a dove in the heart of a child at the next?

Whether the awful claim be true or not, the words have a character of their own, which sets them apart from all other human words, and requires an adequate explanation. Glib suggestions that the man Christ Jesus never uttered them are not enough. For my present argument, it matters not who formed the sentences attributed to Him. As Rousseau said in his Émile: "Never could Jewish writers have found such a tone or such a teaching: in the Gospels are qualities of truth so great, so striking, so totally inimitable that an inventor would be more surprising than he who uttered them."

Four such inventors, all simple, all on the spiritual heights, and all liars, would be more astonishing still. For those who desired to accept the "idea" in detachment from concrete earthly "facts" and historical events (most of them "illusory"), the life of the "Galilean peasant," who had so profoundly affected the world as to rearrange its whole scheme of thought, and the very stones of its architecture, had the symbolical truth of a great poem, in which the most illusory "facts" were themselves curiously perfect parables, or symbolical embodiments of eternal truths.... If we cannot believe that five loaves feed a multitude, we are yet forced to observe that the story is an exquisitely accurate parable of the strange process whereby the mind, heart and spirit of the civilized world have been sustained for nearly two thousand years by the bread of life in one man's word. The very tale is sacramental. The "facts" themselves are the five loaves, and after they are consumed there remain endless fragments of super-substantial Bread. Wherever we touch them they have this virtue. Whether it be the account of an episode, or the record of a word spoken, they had the authenticity and authority of a spiritual law, transcending Nature perhaps, and overruling natural laws, but not contradicting them. Here and now, our water was changed to wine. Here and now the blind were made to see. The "facts," as they were recorded, glowed with an inner light, illuminating the heights and depths of the intellectual and spiritual world. They answered a thousand philosophical riddles, not as the philosopher answers, in empty abstractions, but as the masterpieces of art answer, in their sacramental use of things we daily see and touch and handle.

But these "facts" were not set before us in a masterpiece of art. They were set before us by very simple narrators—whose very earnestness made them fragmentary; yet, when the masters of art have endeavoured to elaborate or glorify or round off those fragments, the simplest words of those humble fishermen have always dwarfed their proudest efforts. Two words of St. John make all the harmonies of Dante and Milton sound like a tinkling cymbal, and one glimpse of the seamless purple at the foot of the Cross brings all the magnificence of Tintoretto down into the dust.

The "facts" were not recorded in masterpieces of art. The symbolism is not planned. It is the natural and inevitable symbolism of facts that accord with and reveal a profound Reality. They were delivered separately by men who were earnestly striving to make a true record of events which they thought of immeasurable importance to their own souls and to the whole world. Whether their attempts be regarded as a failure or not, there is no parallel in the history of the world for so earnest an attempt on the part of four men to make their testimony as to the facts of any event whatsoever. Elaborate histories have been written by scholars. Beautiful legends have been rounded into shape by poets; but of any similar attempt to bear witness, merely for the sake of bearing witness, to a series of alleged facts, for which the testifiers and millions of their followers were ready to offer up their lives, there has been no shadow of a semblance. If those broken narratives, then, had that profound, symbolical, sacramental inner truth, to which the philosophy of Europe has paid its tribute through its deepest minds, there is something more to be accounted for than criticism has yet envisaged. An artless report of the alleged facts can hardly strike deeper than the masterpieces of spiritual and intellectual art, unless there be something more in the "facts" themselves than sceptics are usually prepared to admit.

It seemed possible that they shone with all those strange lights and reflections of the Divine because they themselves actually encompassed and enclosed a Light that our darkness could not comprehend.

The biographical "facts," however, might all be minimized or explained away. The alleged physical miracles all happened long ago and, in every case, even though Hegel decreed the historical Figure to be "unique," they were on *a priori* grounds ruled out by the modern mind.

But this other miracle of the spirit, this Pentecostal flame, shining through all the veils of language and translation, in the four-fold record of the things He said, was there for all to see. The words themselves were a gleam of the divine self-revelation. Even as He speaks the words, He prophesies their power; and the quality of the prophecy can be investigated, here and now, as when He uttered it. *Heaven and earth shall pass away, but My words shall not pass away.*

The values of that utterance—subjected to the coldest standards of literary criticism—are not human. The voice of the Eternal is in it, before whom even the suns and universes dissolve like a shadow, and all the ages of Time are but a moment.

Compare it with any other human utterance, and the immeasurable distance at once appears again, the infinite difference which requires an infinite explanation. Consider, for instance, the words in which that great statesman, Lincoln, expressed the determination of the New World that "government of the people, by the people and for the people shall not perish from the earth." They embody an ideal, and a noble ideal; and yet, compared with those other words, they sound like a tinkling cymbal. They are of the earth, earthy. The political forum echoes in them. It is at least imaginable that someone may have applauded.

The words of Christ are of another order. They are not to be measured by the duration of "the earth." They are of the eternal world, and move us with the strangest apprehension of the human spirit, the sense of *das Heilige.*

And yet—here is the most striking distinction between them. The statesman's utterance appears to be entirely unegotistical. It is concerned with earthly interests, it is true; but they are the interests of "the people." The other utterance appears to be so completely the annunciation of a Self that it dismisses the whole of the rest of the universe as nothing in comparison. In all the utterances of Christ, even in His reassurance of the mourner at the graveside, there is this personal annunciation—*I am the Resurrection and the Life.*

If any other human lips could ever have made a measurable fraction of such a claim it would have sounded like an insane boast. It is only because the claim is not fractional, but complete, that it has never occurred to any one to regard it as a "boast" or as incompatible with a divine humility. The utterance is its own evidence, as no other ever has been; for its kingdom, its infinitude, is within it. Any madman might say things equally impossible from the human point of view; but he could not simultaneously overwhelm us with that strange sense of the infinitely holy, or move the depths of innumerable hearts to adoration for two thousand years by the sheer majesty—and awful humility—of his words. We might also say that the supreme claim of the words would be utterly intolerable if they were not true. But the words have been cherished in the hearts of countless millions, to whom they conveyed the values of God....

This was exactly what had been affirmed by the masterminds of Christendom for nearly twenty centuries, after the most elaborate and profound consideration of all the available facts, by the greatest intellectual and religious councils that the world had ever known. They thought they had an adequate explanation of that constant, profound and solemn mood of the central Figure of religious history, who quietly took His personal identity with the supreme Being for granted, and sometimes directly affirmed it, or with the utmost subtlety implied it, in words that bow the head and break the heart with their beauty. Our immediate conscience almost allowed us to say that, if the affirmation were untrue, it could not have been made in those words. There would have been a false note somewhere, a fault of character, a flaw in the tone; and there is none, even in the broken and stumbling human record. We may be more than sure, therefore, of the original glory of the Aramaic. It is a commonplace of criticism that translation dulls the finer lights and shades of all the masters of literature. Here and there, it is sometimes affirmed that by some rare chance a translator of genius has improved on an inferior original. But in this case there has been no question as to where the original greatness lay, and it shines through four records. It shines, moreover, not only through the Greek, the Latin, and the English, but through every language into which it has been translated, transfiguring even those that are in decadence, with something of its own sacramental splendour.

Taking all these instances together, even this poor literary test gives us a glimpse of the Personality that, across the ages and through all the obstacles of the material world and the dull vesture of our mortality, speaks instantly to what is real in our own personalities, and merely by saying what He says, proves that He has the sole right in the universe to say it....

It was through neglect of these values, which could be perceived here and now, in the actual record, that Renan and so many others went astray. They tried to build up their own independent record, and plunged it in a thousand inconsistencies. Renan's *Vie de Jésus,* that "French novel" as it has justly been called, attempts to depict a beautiful character who is at the same time a despicable impostor; one who could lend himself to a trick at the tomb of Lazarus, and dream of love-affairs in the Garden of Gethsemane. The direct literary test of the values in the Gospels themselves annihilates Renan. Before the fire of one of those burning utterances the romantic creation of Renan shrivels like "a scribbled form, writ on a parchment." It was disregard of the purely "literary test" that so blinded him to the values of character and personality.

There were other definite results that this merely literary test seemed to offer, again and again, and their force was cumulative. No man whose ear had been attuned to great literature could doubt, for instance, that through all the veils of language and translation this proclamation of a unique Self persisted; and that the Voice which said "I am the Resurrection and the Life" was the same as that which said "Be of good cheer, I have overcome the world." It was the same voice that said "I am the vine, ye are the branches," and "Before Abraham was, *I AM.*" Was there ever an assertion like this of a *personal* domination over the relativity of Time?

Those who point to the fact that the assertion of the complete dominion over death occurs only in the fourth Gospel (the most divine of all) are still confronted by equally stupendous implications elsewhere, such as "All power is given unto Me in heaven and on earth"; and "Lo, I am with you all days, even unto the end of the world." If the actual expression in the fourth Gospel is more vitally beautiful, is there not a more vital explanation of this than the suggestion that its author was more of a theologian or philosopher than the writers of the other gospels? To me it seems that we overhear in those ineffable cadences and undertones a direct echo of the living voice which it was natural that the beloved disciple should have caught more perfectly, more profoundly, more exquisitely than another. Its pity had breathed upon him as his head lay upon the divine breast. It is the only adequate explanation of that infinitely tender preparation of his mind for the great farewell, murmuring, with a compassion impossible to man, the consolation that no other could give: "It is expedient for you that I go away.... I will not leave you comfortless. I will come to you."

Let it be regarded from yet another side. Suppose for the moment that the record is really true, and that this "historical Figure approaching us in Time" did indeed embody the "values of God." Nobody with an ear attuned to great literature can doubt for a single moment, in that case, that the words attributed to Him by the simple recorders were absolutely worthy even of Him. The words from the Cross, for instance,

"Forgive them, for they know not what they do," in which the divine Sufferer manifests the divine compassion towards those who nailed Him there, are yet again a proclamation (implied and acted out this time, not asserted) of His own infinitude. But let it be taken with all those other instances, and especially with what is to me the unanswerable instance—*I am the Resurrection and the Life*—and we feel at once that those sentences are perfectly fitting for those divine lips. We should not feel that, in using them, He was falling short of His infinite majesty and holiness.

But it is exactly in the attempt to invent fitting utterance for the Divine—that the masters of merely human expression have always failed. It is one of the commonplaces of literature that even the august spirit of Milton, using the language at perhaps its noblest period, failed and failed miserably in the words that he puts into the mouth of the Son of God. It is a commonplace of criticism that the speeches of his Satan are among the most magnificent ever penned; that, in describing the unattainable light of Heaven he attains sublimity, but that, both in *Paradise Lost* and *Paradise Regained,* except where he directly borrows from the great original, he is utterly inadequate. Thousands can quote line after line of those burning words that he attributes to the fallen archangel. We all remember that courage:

> *"Never to submit or yield,*
> *And what is else not to be overcome."*

But who remembers two consecutive lines of the words that Milton puts into the mouth of the Son of God? There are few who remember a single phrase. The following lines are perhaps the best of them:

> *"I through the ample air in triumph high*
> *Shall lead hell captive, maugre hell, and show*
> *The powers of darkness bound. Thou, at the sight*
> *Pleased, out of heaven shalt look down and smile*
> *While, by thee raised, I ruin all my foes,*
> *Death last, and with his carcase glut the grave."*

They deal with the same subject as what I have called the supreme instance of the Divine utterance in the New Testament; and by a curious accident an exact ground for comparison is offered here. The noblest measure in the English language, the measure into which its finest utterances have fallen as though in accordance with a natural law, is the measure in which Milton wrote his epics, and Shakespeare wrote the greater part of his dramatic works. The greatest line of Shakespeare himself in that measure is perhaps the line in Hamlet, "Absent thee from felicity awhile."

It is merely an accident, from the human point of view, though perhaps in the eternal aspect a breath of inspiration, that an obscure translator, in the age of Shakespeare, should have written, not only the greatest single line in Shakespeare's own measure, but a single line that in itself outweighs all the wonders of his combined works, and compresses more meaning into its ten syllables. It is a line that has been spoken as the final living truth over myriads of graves, and has burned through myriads of desolate minds with a new conviction of immortality. What criticism can fathom that profound calm or explain it?

"I am the Resurrection and the Life." Art and literature are confronted here by a Presence that shrivels them into insignificance; and there is no answer to its instant question—"Whom say *ye* that I am?" but the answer of Peter, "Thou art the Christ, the son of the living God."

THE BOOK OF THE SAVIOUR ꟗ VOLUME TWO

F. J. SHEED

TEACHING UPON THE TRINITY

I

ONE result of reading the Gospels is that we find what Our Lord shows us about God by being God. Another is that we find what Our Lord shows us about God by what He has to say of God.

There is a lot to be said for making one's own list of the texts in which Christ Our Lord tells us of God, grasping them in their context and returning to them again and again. Most of them, naturally, treat of God in His dealings with and judgments of the human race. Save perhaps in the proportion of statements about God's love to statements about His justice, it would be hard to find among these anything that has not already been told us in the Old Testament. There is a new atmosphere, but if it is impossible not to feel the difference, it is almost impossible to lay a precise finger on it—if one happens to know the Old Testament at all well: everything makes us realize how vast a communication about Himself God had already given His chosen people.

In a handful of statements Our Lord covers the ground of the philosophers: God is a spirit (John 4:24); He is perfect (Matt. 5:48); He dwells in secret (Matt. 6:18); He is good and He only (Matt. 19:17); to Him all things are possible (Matt. 19:26); He has never ceased working, that is maintaining creatures in being (John 5:44); He is the one only God (Mark 12:33).

It is a vast reassurance to the mind to have God as it were ratifying the words with which human language has tried to utter Him. It is true that no word of human speech, no concept of the human mind, is adequate; but word and concept are not therefore useless, for God has used them. We may have precious little notion of what they mean in an infinite nature, but the little is precious. They do not give all light, but light-giving they are. God uses them for that.

Our Lord uses them: God had already used them: for not here either do we find anything that is not in the Old Testament. But there is a third sort of statement, which does constitute a new element in God's revelation of Himself to men. As we read what Our Lord tells us of God, we are bound to become conscious of two elements constantly recurring, and recurring in combination—the element of oneness and the element of plurality.

II

I say that this was new. There are in the Old Testament stray hints and gleams of it, but they are no more than that. Thus in the first chapter of Genesis, God says (verse 26), "Let us make man to *our* image and likeness" and in the next verse we read, "And God made man to *his* image and likeness": the plural words "us" and "our" seem to suggest that there were several persons; the singular word "his" that they were somehow one. I do not mean that the human writer of Genesis knew how apt to the reality of God were the words that he wrote: but God Who inspired him knew it. Anyhow, it did not strike the Jews, even by Christ's day, as requiring any special comment. To us again there is something fascinating in the fact that the word for God, "Elohim," is plural: yet it takes a verb in the singular, and if an adjective goes with it, that is in the singular too. But again it did not strike the Jew's, or the Canaanites (who had the same usage) that this had any special significance. Of another sort, there are descriptions of Wisdom which seem to suggest a second person within the Godhead, for example, "And thy wisdom with thee, which knoweth thy works, which then was also present when thou madest the world" (Wis. 9:9). If this is no more than a way of saying that God was not without the attribute of wisdom at the time when He made the world, it seems a rather elaborate way of stating an obvious truth. To us who have heard Our Lord's explicit revelation, such things are full of suggestion. But they did not lead the Jews, nor were they of a sort inescapably to lead them, to the truth that God, remaining one, is yet in some mysterious way more than one. To a truth so astounding indeed, one must be led inescapably or one will not arrive there at all. It is not the sort of truth that one will leap to embrace on a mere hint.

Our Lord did not stop at a hint. As I have said, He insists on an element of plurality, returning to it again and again. There is of course no faintest mitigation of the utter monotheism of the Jews. Our Lord quotes God's own revelation to them: "Hear, O Israel: the Lord thy God is one God." But there is a new element of more-than-oneness, which does not contradict the oneness but somehow enriches it. Thus (John 10:30) He says "I and the Father are One." Here there is clearly a statement of two Who are yet one. In the last two verses of St. Matthew's gospel we find Our Lord saying: "Baptizing them in the name of the Father, and of the Son, and of the Holy Ghost." Here we have plurality again, this time three, yet the unity is stated in the use of the word "name," not "names."

This combination of oneness and plurality is most evident in Our Lord's discourse to the Apostles at the Last Supper. The whole of this discourse, from the fourteenth chapter of St. John to the seventeenth, should be read again and again: everything is in it. But for the moment our concern is with these two elements in what Our Lord has to tell us of the Godhead. In this discourse the special note is what can only be called a certain interchangeability. What I mean by this will appear from some examples. Thus in the fourteenth chapter we find Philip the Apostle saying to Our Lord: "Let us see the Father," and Our Lord answering him, "Whoever has seen me, has seen the Father."

We find this same notion, which I have been driven to call clumsily interchangeability, in what Our Lord has to say of answer to prayer, the sending of the Holy Ghost, God's abiding in our souls. Thus He says (John 16:23): "If you ask the Father anything in my name, he will give it to you." But He had already said (John 14:14): "If you shall ask me anything in my name, that I will do."

We have just heard Our Lord saying that the Paraclete, the Holy Ghost, is to abide with us forever; but a few verses later, in answer to a question of St. Jude, Our Lord says: "If anyone love me he will keep my word and my Father will love him and we will come to him and make our abode with him."

What Our Lord's first hearers, ignorant of the doctrine of the Blessed Trinity, made of His allusions to it we cannot know: we may guess that they were utterly puzzled. But there is a great profit for ourselves, knowing the doctrine, in listening to these same words of Our Lord. I shall not attempt any full treatment here, but shall indicate how the reader may go about it for himself.

Begin with the famous text Matthew 11:27: "No one knows the Son but the Father, and no one knows the Father but the Son, and him to whom the Son shall reveal him."

Here we have two capital points of the doctrine: first, that it can be known only by revelation, the power of the human mind cannot reach it without the aid of God: second, that the central point of the mystery of the relation of Father and Son, that in which its being as a mystery can be summarized, is the knowledge each has of the other—which seems at least to suggest the first procession by way of knowledge.

Self-existence and the timeless present of eternity are in "Before Abraham was made, I am" (John 8:58); equality of nature in "All things whatsoever the Father hath are mine" (John 16:15); distinction of persons and identity of nature in "I and the Father are one" (John 10:30); and that unsayable reality for which theologians have coined the word "circumsession" in "The Father is in me and I in the Father" (John 10:38).

Remembering that nature is the principle of operation—the person does what his nature allows—the identity of nature is asserted by Our Lord in an identity of operation: "My Father works until now and I work" (John 5:17); "Whatsoever things he (the Father) does, these the Son also does in like manner" (John 5:19).

Of the Third Person Our Lord says less; but it is enough. The Spirit is a person: "When *he*, the Spirit of truth is come, he shall lead you unto all truth" (John 16:13); He is equal to the Son, each is a paraclete: "I will ask the Father and he will give you another Paraclete" (John 14:16); He is equal to Father and Son: "baptizing them in the name of the Father and of the Son and of the Holy Ghost" (Matt. 28:19). To see just what that phrase means as to the Godhead of the Holy Ghost, try substituting any other name, however mighty. "In the name of the Father and of the Son and of the Archangel Michael." The thing would sound ridiculous. With all possible respect to the Archangel, one would feel that the company was too exalted for him.

But there is another truth Our Lord makes clear: that though He, the Son, possesses the Divine Nature in total equality with the Father, it is still as a nature received: He is not the origin: "The Son cannot do anything of his own impulse, he can only do what he sees his Father doing" (John 5:19–23) because the Divine Nature in which He lives and moves and has His being is wholly received from His Father.

With this we may compare Our Lord's parallel phrase about the Holy Ghost: "He will not speak of his own impulse, he will utter the message that has been given to him" (John 16:13). For the Holy Ghost, too, has received that Divine Nature which is totally His—received it not from the Father only but from the Son also, so that Our Lord can go on to say: "It is from me that he will derive what he makes plain to you."

This same truth about the procession of the Second Person from the First, and of the Third Person from the First and Second, is illuminated in another way as well. Our Lord speaks of Himself, the Second Person, as being "sent"—always by the Father. He speaks of the Third Person as to be sent—sometimes by the Father, sometimes by Himself. In this "sending" we must see no glimmer of subordination of the Son and the Holy Spirit. They come to us by the divine will, which is their own as totally as it is the Father's: but inasmuch as they received the nature in which that will is, they may be thought of as sent. That is why the Father, who possesses the Divine Nature as unreceived, is never spoken of as sent; that is why the Son, who receives the Divine Nature from the Father alone, is spoken of as sent by the Father but not by the Holy Ghost; that is why the Holy Ghost, who receives the Divine Nature from Father and Son, is spoken of as sent by the Father and by the Son. But it must be repeated, the sending is not to be thought of as a command imposed but as the free decision of a nature possessed in total equality by each.

HENRY CONSTABLE

TO GOD THE FATHER

Great God: within whose simple essence, we
nothing but that which is Thy Self can find;
when on Thyself thou didst reflect Thy mind,
Thy thought was God, which took the form of Thee:
And when this God thus born, Thou lov'st, and He
lov'd Thee again, with passion of like kind,
as lovers' sighs which meet become one mind,
both breath'd one Spirit of equal deity.
Eternal Father, whence these two do come
and wil'st the title of my father have,
an heavenly knowledge in my mind engrave,
That it Thy Son's true Image may become:
incense my heart with sighs of holy Love
that it the temple of the Spirit may prove.

C. C. MARTINDALE, S.J.

LIFE AND THE FOOD OF LIFE

I

We come to what our Lord regards as the supreme topic of His proclamation, and, indeed, as the very object of His coming amongst us and of His existence. He had said: "I am come to seek and to save that which was lost." But when you ask: "What will you do then? For *what* are you saving them? He answers: "I am come that they might have life and have it more abundantly" (John 10:10). And if one asks: "What do you mean by *life*?" He replies (as by now you might expect): "*I* am the Life."

Now, to these words we have most emphatically to attach a meaning. Were you to say to anyone: "Christ is my life," or even, "Christ is Life," you would be thought a fanatic or mad. And you would indeed be hard put to it to explain what you did mean. Yet both those sentences would, on the lips of Christians, be perfectly sensible things to say, and, indeed, the only thing that a Christian in the last resort could say.

What do you mean, anyway, by "life"? Baffling question, if you really seek an answer. A word that is used by us all so glibly; that has entered into a thousand habitual phrases and even slang. "I want to see life," says the lad emancipated from his school and embarking on a tour round the world, or even round London after dark. "Music is my life!" cries the enthusiast, implying at least that every other mode of existence in which music played no part would be intolerable, and that without music she would at once commit suicide. "I have lived my life," sighs the elderly person who envies the opportunities and zest of youth; and the prize-fighter announces that life for him is over in his thirties. Moreover, life is dear. Again and again I have seen men in war-hospitals, of whom you honestly thought that it would be better that they should die—limbs shot away; face shot away. But they would say to one: "Life is very precious, Father." What could they mean?

Let us begin by acknowledging that we do see a difference between the most perfect imitation and the simplest living thing. Nay, you can have a silken flower or a waxen fruit that *would be* far finer specimens of what they represent than the actual tulip, the actual peach that is in your possession, *were they real.* They have not and cannot have that mysterious interior glow, pulsation, activity—that power of taking up other things and turning them into their living selves that is so different from mere absorption; that casting of their unity of Self-hood over what they assimilate, but, above all, that radiant Beauty which is proper to vitality and which we can never never make nor give. I confess that I am lost in worship before the simplest living thing, because by that fact of life I enter into all but direct communication with the Creator of all Life whatsoever. I know that even "lifeless" things possess reality and energy, and neither can these be created by me or by anyone else; but at least I can shift the earth about and remodel stones and interconnect them in such ways as they permit; but they do not grow; they do not develop; they are not alive, and while I can destroy life I cannot even seem to supply it.

Such life is not its own absolute justification. It is no sin to pick a flower and see it wilt when the due hours have passed. Nor yet to kill a bird, a rabbit. But I confess that when I see, for example, a shot pheasant, and in an instant its vivid black eye filmed, the glow and gloss gone in but a moment from its feathers, the thing *taken* that can never be given nor restored... I confess to feeling that I would hesitate long before doing any such thing as to kill. I frankly acknowledge this, alien as it is to our national instinct for "sport," and superficially similar as it seems to the doctrine of those who say you have no right thus to kill, which is false. But it remains that for no merely selfish reason would I ever wish to see dead that which is capable of life.

Now, if I can thus go to communion with God in the grass of the field, the least little living insect, what must I think when I come to man?

Human life can be a terrifying thing to think of. I don't mean the incidents or conditions of such or such a life, but the thing itself. Its egocentricity. By that I mean that each man is the centre of his whole world. He describes everything in terms of himself, so far as its position goes. Two men face one another, and one will say that a thing is on his left, while the other must needs say that it is on his right. Each occupies his little bit of space in this world, and while he is there no one else can be there, and from there he looks out at the entire universe. But what is his bodily position, despite its uniqueness, when compared with the lonely independence of his mind? Each man sees through his own eyes; each thinks his own thoughts, unshared by any other. For you may learn from your neighbour what he thinks, but you cannot think *his* thoughts, nor feel *his* feelings. Even when you know another well, and love him or her most intimately, and as it were live by that other's life and have one soul between you—all that is, after all, but a way of speaking, and for ever and for ever you are not that other, but your Self. Each person who reads this book is thinking special thoughts—isolated thoughts—about what is read; a barrier as of ice—impenetrable more than ice is, even though transparent, maybe, as purest ice—separates each reader from every other reader, and only by the bridge of words, or of imagination, or of guess, can any one soul communicate—and even then how partially—with any other soul! God-like and majestic uniqueness of each soul! And pathetic isolation of each soul—limitations of each soul—loneliness of each soul! Life itself is so marvellous that it may almost steal the worship due to God, and, indeed, in pagan ages the myriad phenomena of Life did so steal it. But when you realize the tininess of each human life, the small scope of its awareness, its wavering will, how tragic would be such a god-hood, if god-hood indeed it were! Enough. As life it is amazing, and a contact with God, but how different from God—how much is it *not*, that God *is*.

II

Because, then, of the mysterious magnificence of this thing, and because of its insufficiency, Christ says that He means to give us more of it, and for that purpose has He come. The whole Gospel of St. John is occupied with this theme of Life—Life of which our Lord says to Nicodemus that it needs to be given to a man from God, for, how can a man bring himself alive? Yet we need to be "born anew." And, speaking with the Samaritan woman, He pictures it as a fountain leaping ever fresh within the soul. And then He works the "sign" that shall enable Him to speak still more definitely about it. He heals the paralytic man—restores him, as we might say, to life—and, when they stand astonished, He proclaims that greater works than this shall He show them, that then, indeed, they may marvel. For, as the Father can raise the dead and give life to them, so, too, the Son—whom He wills, them maketh He alive. "He," our Lord continues, "who hears My word and believes in Him who sent Me *hath* eternal life... he has crossed over from Death into Life." We have to "hear Him," in a way that will mean more than merely listen to Him; "see Him," so that we are not just looking at Him; "come to Him," so that we somehow adhere to Him and are not just standing alongside of Him; "believe in Him" in a way that surpasses the mere regarding what He says as true; and then something will happen to us which is no more than palely shadowed forth by the restoration of paralyzed limbs to the ordinary energies of man, and what can but be described as a "making alive," as though all our earlier vitality had been but death.

Does our Lord, indeed, mean just physical resuscitation? Well, recall the incident of Lazarus. Lazarus had died and for four days had been buried. Our Lord raised him to bodily life again. That, surely, would be one of those "greater things" at which "indeed we might marvel"? Recall what had passed between our Lord and the dead man's sister, Martha. "Oh, if you had been here," the poor woman in her anguish cried to Him, "my brother had not died." "Thy brother," He answered, "shall rise again." "I know that he shall rise," she said, despondently, "at the last day." Ah, no! Even that, even that mysterious restoration to "life" that is to befall every one of us, is but a material affair, itself little more than a symbol of that Giving of Life that is the purpose of Christ amongst us. So you hear now from His lips the tremendous identification:

"I am the Resurrection and the Life;
He that believeth in Me, though he were dead,
shall live;
And he that liveth, and believeth in Me
shall never die."

I cannot here rehearse the whole of the doctrine of Grace. I can only say that as a stone is not alive at all, and as a flower "lives," yet with how slender and semi-real a life compared to the meanest among animals, and as it would be death for a man were all that is peculiarly human in him—intelligence and freedom of will—to be stricken from him and he reduced to be but as the brutes are, so there is a yet higher life in store for men, a supernatural life, a free gift from God and called, therefore, "grace"—for that is what grace means. And the plan of God is that we should acquire that life by incorporation with our Lord, so that by His life we live. This is not altogether beyond our imagination or understanding, because you may have experienced how you can actually absorb vitality from proximity to a very vitalized and healthful person, and how exhausted you can become by much dealing with a fatigued or bloodless person—someone who is, as they say, but half-alive—dead-and-alive. And you can also recognize how great is our increase of vitality by sheer social life, by incorporation with our fellows in a "side," a party, any group animated by one thought and will. A new personality springs into being—the collective vitality of the group, in which we share and which invigorates and reinforces us. Dim, indeed, are these comparisons for the illustrating of what happens when you come into contact—personal, vital, organic contact with Jesus Christ, our Life.

III

"Come to Me—I am the Bread. I am the Vine!" I remind you briefly of the way in which our Lord made His great proclamation of Himself as our food (John 6). He led up to it, as ever, gradually.

First, He worked the miracle of the multiplication of the loaves, meaning to use that miracle as the taking-off point, so to say, for His further spiritual doctrine. The crowds certainly flocked together on the next day, but He had to rebuke them—they had come out of astonishment, excitement—they did not even see that the miracle was a "sign," that is, that it pointed to something beyond itself. Unless they *could* get further than this material food, and even than the exterior miracle, they need not have troubled thus to throng to Him.

> *"Work not," He cried, "for the food that perishes,*
> *But for the Food that endures unto Eternal Life—*
> *The Food that the Son of Man is offering you:*
> *For Him hath the Father sealed, even God."*

"What are we to do," they answer, "that we may work
'Works of God'?"

"This is the Work of God—
To believe in Him whom God hath sent."

They realize that He is making the supreme claim to be the Messiah. In what sense would He work, or had He worked, a "sign" that should convince them of that?

"What sign workest Thou, that we may see it,
And put Faith in Thee?
Our forefathers did eat the Manna in the wilderness—
'He gave them bread from heaven to eat...'
What workest Thou?"
"In solemn truth I tell you—
Not Moses gave you the real Bread from Heaven;
But my Father is offering you the Bread from Heaven—
The True Bread.
For the Bread of God
Is that which comes down out of Heaven
And gives life to the world."

The Jews do not immediately see that "That which came down out of heaven" is one and the same thing as "He who came down out of heaven"; and, half clumsily, like the woman at the well, who asked our Lord to give her His mysterious spring-water, so that she need trouble no more to come and draw laborious pailfuls from this well, they cry: "Give us this bread always!" He has to speak more clearly.

"I am the Bread of Life:
He who cometh unto Me
Shall never hunger;
And he who believeth in Me
Shall thirst no more at all."

And He repeats and insists that it is He who has come down from heaven, for no private purposes of His own, so to say, but to accomplish the Father's will, that is, the giving of life to a dead world. But now the Jews are indignant. They knew, said they, His parents. How, then, could He have come down out of heaven? Our Lord insists but the more:

"I am the Bread of Life.
Your forefathers ate the Manna in the wilderness,
And died.
This is the Bread that comes down out of heaven,
That a man may eat of that
And never die.
I am the Living Bread
Which comes down out of heaven;

If a man eat of My Bread
He shall live for ever.
And the Bread that I will give for the world's life
Is My Flesh."

Observe the steps by which Christ has moved. Do not exhaust yourselves by working merely for this world's life. Work God's works, proper to a diviner life.—How can we do that?—By believing in Me.—What, then, are your credentials, your heavenly guarantee, equivalent to the manna given by Moses—"bread from heaven"?—That bread-from-heaven gave no real life. My Father is offering—is sending—a true Bread from Heaven, that Bread of Life. Come to Me—believe in Me—eat of it—eat of Me—and live "eternally"! Yes—feed on *Me*. For that Bread is My Flesh.

Like Nicodemus, who, on hearing that men must be "born anew," asked "How can these things be?" the Jews wrestle with the problem: "How can this man give us His flesh to eat?"

Our Lord, with ever growing emphasis, repeats His assertion, in negative form at first, then, positive and triumphant.

"In solemn truth I tell you—
If you do not eat the Flesh of the Son of Man,
And do not drink His Blood,
You have no Life in you.
He who doth eat My Flesh

And drink My Blood,
Hath Eternal Life…
For My Flesh is a true food,
And My Blood, true drink:
He that eateth My Flesh
And drinketh My Blood
Abideth in Me,
And I in him.

As it was He, the Living Father, who did send Me,
So he that eateth Me
He shall live, too, by Me.
This is the Bread that came down out of heaven:
Not as your fathers ate,
And died,
He who eateth this Bread
Shall live for ever."

VINCENT MCNABB, O.P.

TEACHING UPON THE LAW

Central in Our Blessed Lord's teaching, because central in the political and religious life of the little people whom He taught, was the question of the Law. It was the unique achievement of this little God-guided people that no other pre-Christian people, small or great, had explicitly and minutely based, as they had based, their social code on an ethical code. Not even Greece, of the golden age of Plato's Republic and Aristotle's Nicomachean Ethics, had attempted what the Jews before them had attempted and achieved. Indeed, far from seeking to measure the State by an immovable or absolute ethical code, these Greek thinkers were bewildered into finding the ethical absolute in the State itself. For the Greeks, with their merely notional acceptance of God and their very definite patriotic acceptance of Greece, the good man was the good citizen. On the other hand, for the Jew, with his concept of God clearer than even his clear patriotic concept of his nation, the good man, being God's man, would necessarily be the good citizen.

The Jewish law consisted of general precepts and of particular precepts.

The general precepts were a fundamental ethical code. They were called the Decalogue or Ten Commandments. By later writers they are called the Moral Precepts.

This fundamental ethical code of moral precepts contained only the general, as distinct from the particular, duties of man to God, and of man to his fellow-men. To these general moral precepts were added particular precepts: (1) The ceremonial precepts dealing with man's duties to God; and (2) The social or judicial precepts, dealing with man's duties to his fellow-men.

We need not remark that the fundamental ethical code was unchangeable. But the ceremonial precepts, which were preparatory for the coming of the Messiah, were unchangeable only until He came. His coming would necessarily make their continuance an untruth.

Again, the social precepts, which were laws made for the civic life of the Jewish people, and therefore not adapted to every people, had neither the essential continuance of the moral precepts, nor the essential discontinuance of the ceremonial precepts, but might or might not be continued according to the will of a people.

As there was no direct effect of Our Blessed Lord's action that was not part of His plan, we now know that He was minded (1) to support the ethical precepts of the Law; (2) to abolish the (preparatory) ceremonial precepts of the Law; and (3) to leave untouched the social precepts of the Law.

Perhaps we have not yet recognized how Our Blessed Redeemer's support of the precepts of the Natural Law mark Him off from the few men whom many of their fellow-men look on as religious leaders. Men as strong-minded as Muhammad did not feel themselves strong enough to impose sexual ethics beyond the average of their contemporaries. On the other hand, Jesus found a level of morality which it would have been easy enough, and worldly-prudent enough, *not* to follow. For example, though there had been no legal repeal of the precept "Thou shalt not commit adultery," there was such a widespread practical repeal that the legal machinery for punishing adultery by stoning the adulteress had long since ceased to function.

Lesser moralists, such as the world has often seen, would have acted on the principle: "The precept has been universally denied in practice. Let us avoid hypocrisy—let us deny it in principle." Our Blessed Lord's avoidance of this wonted way of popularity for religious reformers argues a wisdom beyond that of the worldly-wise.

This reinforcement of the moral precepts of the Law made Him many friends, especially among the simple, God-fearing people. But it also made Him many and perhaps more enemies amongst those who, like the Pharisee of the parable, thought themselves God-fearing people. If not all of them felt the lash of His denunciation of fornication and adultery, they could not help feeling scourged with thongs of truth when He spoke of honouring father and mother, and pilloried those whose tithing of mint and cumin was a breach of "Thou shalt not steal."

But if Our Blessed Lord's reinforcement of the moral precepts of the Law recruited His enemies heavily from the wicked, His abrogation of the ceremonial precepts made many enemies even of the good. These good men could see only as Sabbatarians. Their Sabbath, with its elaborate ritual, was such a national, religious, historic, artistic social synthesis and symbol that any change in it was worse than sedition. Indeed, because whoever ventured to change an institution as divine as the Sabbath claimed to be divine, it seemed to follow that Jesus, by claiming authority over the Sabbath, was implicitly claiming to be equal to God. No wonder there is a note of understanding, if not sympathy, in Our Lord's words to His apostles: "The hour cometh when whosoever killeth you will think he offereth a sacrifice to God."

These good folk, with headlong zeal for the Sabbath, did not take time to realize that it was not the substance but the passing accompaniments of the ceremonial law which Jesus was minded to abrogate. It was not sacrifice, but the lesser sacrifices of living and lifeless beings, He was abrogating. Indeed, He was preparing to fulfil and perfect all local sacrifices by the unique self-sacrifice of the Cross. So little of what was permanent was ended that His Apostles have transmitted to all time the weekly sacrifice, and have laid upon their followers the duty of assisting at that weekly sacrifice under pain of grievous sin. It is even arguable that if the Catholic obligation of presence at the weekly sacrifice were to fail, the very notion of man's individual and collective duty of sacrifice to God would perish in the world. It was not then the substance, but some of the ceremonial accompaniments of sacrifice that were set aside when Jesus showed Himself Master of the Sabbath. But, as preparations for the king's coming are set aside when the king has come, so were the elaborate legal ceremonies preparatory to the coming of the Messiah set aside when Jesus, the Messiah, had come.

If we have ventured to suggest that Our Blessed Lord's attitude to the moral precepts and the ceremonial precepts of the Law argued, or at least evidenced, a more than human wisdom, that wisdom is corroborated by His attitude towards the social precepts of the Law. Circumstances which would have led any other reformer into political action for the good of his religious reform left Jesus untouched. The occupation of a religious reformer's country by a foreign nation is an opportunity for giving his reform the cutting-edge of patriotism. Even nowadays moral reformers commonly denounce the immorality of their country as a foreign import. The Roman occupation of Palestine gave Our Blessed Lord an unique opportunity of enlisting the whole force of Jewish patriotism on the side of His religious mission. What that patriotism was capable of could be measured by the battlings and victories of the Maccabees. Even as He went from hamlet to hamlet a group of His fellow-Galileans—perhaps after hearing His words—had made an appeal to the sword and had soon experienced the terrible Roman wrath, the ruthless guardian of the Roman peace.

CARYLL HOUSELANDER

MATTHEW SPEAKS

I

His fame had spread through Syria like flame in dry grass,
From Galilee and the Decapolis and over Jordan the
people came.
Crowds came out of Judea and out of Jerusalem.

In the hearts of the old men
hope for the race smouldered again:
"Oh, that Messiah were come to set us free!"
In the hearts of the women
hope for the children flickered with faint flame:
"Oh, that Messiah were come to set them free!"
The proud heart of youth blazed, suddenly on fire:
"Oh, for our own glory, in the glory of Messiah!"

I was afraid,
I, the tax-collector,
who had sat in the custom house.
I knew men through and through,
having got my living, as it were,
by other men's despair.

I knew the humiliated,
I knew the oppressed;
I knew the king.
whom they had crowned already
in their desire:
they had created him
out of their bitterness.

Out of their broken flesh,
out of their hunger and thirst,
out of their chains—
weaponless, they had forged him a sword;
ragged, they had woven for him
purple raiment and cloth of gold for a king:
out of the festering wound, out of the conqueror's scorn,
in dreams, the son of the race was born—
Messiah, the Son of Dreams.

I knew it all.
How often I had sat in the market-place
and seen the women there, rocking to and fro,
like those who sit by the dead to weep—
rocking, rocking, rocking,
to and fro;
trying to rock the cradled nothingness
in the barren womb
to sleep.

As for the young,
they wanted a leader, whose power
would be in his lust for power,
one whose tongue
would utter their dumb pride
in song,
one in whose heart
their frightened hearts would beat
to the sound of drums.

II

I was afraid
that they would despair
when they saw the Lord.

He was very poor,
He had the chiselled features
of one who denies himself;
His hands
were the large hands
of an artisan—
and without a sword;
His eyes,
the eyes of pity and love;
His speech,
the broad, slow speech
of a countryman.

I was afraid,
But when He began to speak
it seemed to each who heard
that the word was spoken to him alone.

He dawned upon the people;
He did not take them by storm:
soft as the blown thistledown's sowing,
the seed of the Word was sown.

Each who heard
knew the light growing within him,
like morning,

slowly welling
and filling the empty sky
before the first song
of the first bird.

I understood,
when He began to teach,
why first
He had given light to blind eyes;
and to deaf ears,
the music of water and wind;
and to hands and feet that were numb,
the touch of the delicate grass and the sun;
and speech to the dumb.

For He spoke of the things
men see and taste and hold:
of salt and rock and light
and the wheat in gold;
of winds and wings and flowers
and the fruit on boughs;
of candle-light in the house.

They heard His voice,
Like the voice of a murmurous sea
a long way off, washing the shores of peace:

but each knew within him
a soundless music,
a voiceless singing, saying:

"Feel the pulse of My love
with your finger-tips;
prove My tenderness
in the tiny beat
of the heart of the mother bird;
lay your hand on the hard bark of the tree—
know Me
in the rising sap
of the green life
in the dark.

"I have strewn the flowers
under your feet:
see if I love you:
see if My love is sweet!"

There was a thawing then,
like the melting of frost
when winter is done
and the warm sun
kisses the world.

THE PROCLAMATION OF THE KINGDOM

There was a thawing then
in the hearts of the women,
and after the hard frost
of the hard years,
their unshed tears
were flowing.

They understood
how the Lord
takes the loveliest least
for His self-bestowing.

They would remember,
when they were baking bread,
how He had said
that His grace
works secretly in them,
like yeast.

When they sifted the ash
and blew the spark of the fire,
they would remember
the Breath of the Spirit
that fans the smoking flax.

He spoke of chastity,
the splendour of love;
of desire,
silver purified
in the heart of the fire;
of thought,
white linen spread
for the marriage feast.

Then
the men knew,
with a great sighing of joy,
that the dead bough
must fall from the living tree;
the fetid thought,
the furtive word,
the seeping lust,
the cloying grief,
the blight on the green leaf,
the hard fruit
with soft rot at the core,
would be no more,
no more.
But the heart would be born again
to a white maying and morning
and first falling in love.

III

Christ looked at the people.
He saw them assailed by fear:
He saw the locked door;
He saw the knife in the hand;
He saw the buried coin;
He saw the unworn coat,
consumed by moth;
He saw the stagnant water
drawn and kept in the pitcher,
the musty bread in the bin—
the defended,
the unshared,
the ungiven.

He told them then
of the love
that casts out fear,
of the love that is four walls
and a roof over the head:
of the knife in the sheath,
of the coin in the open hand,
of the coin given
warm with the giver's life,
of the water poured in the cup,
of the table spread—

the undefended,
the shared,
the given—
the Kingdom of Heaven.

Christ looked at the people.
He saw the hard years
graven upon their faces;
He saw the old clothes,
worn to the shape of their work;
He saw their unshed tears;
He saw the labourer's hands,
hollowed out by the tools
as His own were hollowed out
by the mallet to cup the nail.

He saw the crust of the will,
like the hard crust of rye;
He saw flesh and blood,
the sacramentals of love;
He saw the image of God,
the crystal in the rock.

He lifted
His large and beautiful hands
to bless.

P. R. RÉGAMEY, O.P.

TEACHING UPON POVERTY

I

THE Son of God expected those who served His Father to welcome Him, and it was for them that He came. When He opened the prophecy of Isaiah in the synagogue at Nazareth, He chose this passage: "The spirit of the Lord is upon me. Wherefore he hath anointed me to speak the gospel to the poor: he hath sent me to heal the contrite of heart. To preach deliverance to the captives and sight to the blind, to set at liberty them that are bruised, to preach the acceptable year of the Lord and the day of reward. And when he had folded the book he restored it to the minister and sat down. And the eyes of all in the synagogue were fixed on him." Then He spoke with authority, "This day is fulfilled this scripture in your ears."

When He had before Him the crowd of the poor, the crippled, the unfortunates of all sorts who had followed Him into His solitude, He raised His eyes to them, says St. Luke—we can imagine with what love—and cried out: "Blessed are ye poor." It was as though the whole meaning of His message lay in that: You have no idea how lucky you are! I have come to tell you, I have brought you the good news! At His birth, His first thought was for a group of poor men: He had sent an angel to the shepherds nearby to tell them from Him: "I bring you good tidings of great joy." And in case John the Baptist might be astonished at His puzzling way of revealing Himself, instead of making the glitter expected of the Messiah, He answered His forerunner's disciples: Go and relate to John what you have heard and seen; the blind see, the lame walk, the lepers are made clean, the deaf hear, the dead rise again, to the poor the gospel is preached." The sentence clearly rises past the raising of the dead to a climax, to a kind of miracle still more amazing than those first mentioned. Does it not imply that it is even more extraordinary for the poor to have the gospel preached to them than for the dead to be raised again? I find it hard not to think so. In any case, the last phrase is certainly not the once exception in a list made up of miracles.

To announce the gospel to the poor is, surely, the hardest thing of all, for it is making them see that for them happiness consists in being poor.

Our Lord then preached by example. He chose to live in a nation that had lost its heritage, during a tragic period of its history. Christians do not give enough thought to the conditions in which He lived. They picture the charming scenes at

Galilee, or the simplicity of His life with the fishermen of the lake, without seeing the darker colours of His country and His time. Palestine cut a sad figure in human eyes beside Tyre and the great empires nearby. And by the time God came to live there, she had long been trampled underfoot by the nations. The Syrians, the Egyptians, the Chaldeans, the Assyrians, the Greeks and the Romans had all ravaged her. She was an occupied country and her conquerors were harsh.

What are the estimates of historians worth? One says: "If one reckoned up all those who fell during the wars and revolutions and added those assassinated by the orders of Herod and the procurators, during that dreadful century, the total would be at least two hundred thousand men—a terrifying number for so small a country, and even more terrifying when one considers that those who died on the battlefields were the physical elite of the nation, and Herod's victims represented the intellectual elite." It is hard to see how we can establish even an approximate figure, but the impressions of the scholars do call up a picture of the misery and suffering in which Christ chose to live His life so totally. That was the context—it was to those men at that time and in that country that He was preaching the blessedness of poverty, and of tears, of gentleness and peace. And that is the tone of the Gospel.

How great was Christ's personal poverty in this impoverished time? The indications given us by the Gospel are like the remains of a very old painting; men who cannot understand them tear them apart wondering how they can be compatible, never realising what the atmosphere of those early days was really like. On one side you have the birth in the stable, then later the accusation that He loves good meat and good wine, an accusation which must have had some sort of basis; and at the heart of everything the frightful abjection of His Passion and Cross. I know that mediocre men will always explain the Gospel according to their own mediocre ideals; they see Jesus leading a simple life of moderate means, with certain privations and trials, no doubt, but on the whole realising an average degree of comfort, without excess in either direction until the Passion. On the other hand there are tormented imaginations which see it all as tragic. Examine the facts carefully, hear what the exegetes have to say, try to bring the whole thing alive—you can do this because of the "sense of Christ" Our Lord inspires in the faithful through the Church—and you will not be able to accept either interpretation. You must somehow unite them—going further in both directions!

For the compass of Christ is always a union of extremes. We can never exaggerate the position the Cross held in His mind. It obsessed Him all His life with a strength that was the strength of His love. A single glimpse of the "furnace" that His heart was, and of the wealth of the suffering He chose to undergo, makes it clear that even when His way of living looked like any other man's the work of the Spirit must have been intense. If He was placing Himself within our limits, He was doing so with an infinite ardour. As His Transfiguration manifested for a moment the glory whose splendour was always with Him, so the astonishing destitution He underwent revealed His passionate thirst for poverty. But while the Transfiguration was a single incident, which He showed to only three witnesses, He continually and openly suffered extreme humiliations because He had become man, and must touch the depths of man's miseries. However low we fall, we will always find Him lower. But with His immense liberty of soul, He would not be restricted to one single line. He took advantage of riches where He found them, visiting Levi, Zachaeus, and Simon, honouring their meals by the very sharing of them. He was too utterly poor to consider poverty an absolute value: He was detached even from poverty. Possessing every perfection, He must have been able to say with even more right than His apostle: "I have learned in whatsoever state I am to be content therewith. I know both how to be brought low, and know how to abound (everywhere and in all things I am instructed): both to be full and to be hungry: both to abound and to suffer need" (Phil. 4:11–12). St. Paul concludes: "I can do all things, in him who strengthened me." How much more, then, was Christ Himself, the Author of that strength, wholly independent alike of possessions and privations.

He was born in a stable, and while we must see all that centuries of Christian meditation have seen in the fact, we must also realise that this solitary and sheltered place was far less painful than the crowding, the vulgarity, the noise of the caravanserai, where His parents could find no room. Nazareth was thought a wretched little place; its name appears neither in the Old Testament nor the rabbinical writings, and we find it said, "Can anything of good come from Nazareth?" Its houses were rather hollowed out of the crumbling rock than built up from without, and the air in them was the air of a cellar. But the earth was fertile, the harvests yielded a hundredfold, there was abundance of olive oil, and Joseph the carpenter cannot have had much trouble in making a living for himself and his family. The people were slow-witted and violent. As in our own lives, bitter and sweet were mixed inextricably in everything. You have not got to see the picture as one of unrelieved blackness. Tragedy lives far below the outer crust of experience.

Just before Our Lord began His ministry, the devil tempted Him to turn His spiritual wealth to material profit: to turn stones into bread. He replied, as He was so often to insist later, that God's word was enough—so much so that by a sort of over-measure or "bonus" it even sustained physical life. But this trust in God's help remained within the framework of the needs God willed and never became rash or presumptuous. "It is written: thou shalt not tempt the Lord thy God." And lastly, He refused the earthly power and glory offered Him. He triumphed by abasing Himself to adore God.

We see Him next as a preacher, and He shows at once the selflessness of the apostle. Now this was more than just a necessary means, something called for by the very nature of apostleship. Our Lord parted company with His mother. She hastened the hour of parting herself, by asking Him to perform His first miracle, at Cana. He showed that He was God, Lord of the elements. He left her, denied Himself her companionship, because He had a task to perform as the Word of God. And when she followed Him (perhaps because the anguish became too keen, or perhaps giving way to the entreaties and complaints of His cousins), He seemed absolutely to repel her. Mary then disappears from the gospel, and we do not see her again till Calvary, where she completes her sacrifice with her Son's.

He tramped the roads. He often spent whole nights in prayer in the wilderness. He had no home, "Nowhere to lay his head." One day He had no money to pay the tribute for Himself and Peter, and the only thing to do was to perform a miracle to get the drachma they needed. However, do not let us exaggerate. The apostles had a purse which Judas had charge of, and it must generally have been full, since Judas found in it something to steal, and when they were in unfriendly country, they did not depend on what they were given, but bought food. There were holy women, some of them rich, who devoted themselves to Christ and His disciples and helped them. He took pleasure in being entertained in at least one household—Bethany; there they went to such trouble for Him that He begged for more simplicity: "One dish is enough" (that was the immediate meaning of the "one thing necessary"—surely so homely a phrase never had such spiritual resonances!). He opened His heart quite naturally to friendship.

These very human characteristics, together with those mentioned earlier, take on fullness of meaning when we remember that Our Lord came to give us an example of detachment, when we know that He knew "what was in men's hearts," when we see everything, as we must, in the light of the Passion. He saw every detail of it with His divine knowledge, His own prophetic sight of the future, and the writings of the prophets who had announced His coming. Towards the Passion He went with an anguish that made Him groan, and yet with an unutterable longing (John 12:27). That was why He was here. "But for this cause I came unto this hour." During this "hour" His actions had a redemptive power, not so much because they were what they were as because He offered them for us with infinite love. He could have saved the world by any one of them, but Eternal Wisdom willed this frightful overabundance of suffering and humiliation; the reason, I suppose, was to give this love full scope for its ardour, and to bring men to realise the near frenzy of it. It was suffering indeed, and Christians should strive to understand it, though they can never see it clearly or sorrowfully enough. But it was even more a stripping off of everything—utter abandonment. The Passion was the collapse of the great hope, a failure made shameful by the gibes of men. It was a tearing away of everything even down to His clothes, in Latin, *habitus,* what we *have,* what is most clearly ours, the last thing left us as long as anything is left us at all. When we reach the point of losing even our clothes, then we have certainly lost the most fundamental of the gifts we *can* lose, our dignity. We are brought down to our very essence. But Christ knew the most mysterious dereliction of all. He was betrayed by His friends, reduced to the state of a criminal slave, "delivered into the hands of men"—and nothing could be more terrible than that: in the instability of the world today, when no barrier seems to stand against human cruelty, we begin to see what it means to be delivered into the hands of men. Men, furious at the disappointment of their hopes, made a mock of Christ, cast Him out of their world, thrust Him up towards Heaven on a cross.

II

St. Paul says that for *us* Christ, who was richness itself, became poor (1 Cor. 8:9). Christ's teaching—being at once extreme and moderate—is as complex as His example. We can only realise its perfect oneness by an impulse of the Holy Ghost. Anyone with no sense of eternal life will find it contradictory. There are critics who see in it two irreconcilable doctrines. Men who can see no further than this world are short-sighted, and cannot see into the distance where they meet. On the one hand, they see Our Lord violently condemning riches, on the other simply giving in to the accepted state of things in a world founded on them.

"Woe to you that are rich...." "It is easier for a camel (or a cable, says another translation), to pass through the eye of a needle, than for a rich man to enter into the kingdom of heaven." Money is called "the mammon of iniquity." In this regard, Jesus, usually so gentle, appears far harsher when it comes to the point than His terrible cousin, John the Baptist. The precursor, when it came to practical questions, was quite moderate. He shook the crowd by the force with which he spoke, but when they asked in fear and trembling, "What then? ... What must we do?", he simply replied that they must share out their goods, so that what the rich had above their needs might be given to those who had needs to fill. Dealing with the publicans and soldiers—both of whose jobs involved extorting money—he did not even order them to right the wrongs they had done; he simply said to them: "Do nothing more than that which is appointed you.... Do violence to no man.... Be content with your pay." Whereas Jesus answered: "Go sell what thou hast and give to the poor."

He snatched the tax-collector away from his counter. And if anyone objected: "How then is a man to live?", His answer, at least as some have seen it, was: "Only the baser sort worry about that."

And yet, it has also been argued that He was willing to accommodate Himself to the conventions of property as they were seen, by the world of His day. So much so that a whole system of conservative morality has been formulated from the gospel; more or less like this: (1) It is not indispensable for the rich to give away all their goods (Matt. 10:42). (2) Property must be respected (Luke 16:11; 20:14; 15:12). (3) It is perfectly legitimate to let out to rent, to trade, to lend at interest, to make money (Matt. 25:16). (4) A certain prudent self-interest is praiseworthy (Matt. 23:44; 18:34; 25:14). (5) Christ promised material riches to all who believed (Luke 18:29).

Looking at these two groups of facts and teachings, the modern man who wonders whether Christ was a capitalist or a communist comes to the conclusion that there is simply no way of reconciling His teachings.

Loisy finds his own way out: he thinks that Our Lord expected the world to end very shortly, and therefore thought that none of it mattered very much. All he thought necessary was a sort of "interim morality."

Now we know that Christ founded His Church to last for all the centuries, and we also know that during all those centuries, material realities have been enormously important, their influence truly immeasurable. How? Beyond our line of vision. And not in their own right, but rather because of the heart that is fixed on them.

What Christ is really saying is that riches and poverty have no value in themselves. What matters is how we treat them. We have got to use our earthly life to get beyond this earth. We are at work to establish the Kingdom of God here as far as we can, which means that the realities of this world must be transfigured, but first we must, so to speak, turn them round. Our point of view is divine, our object is divine, but our material is the realities of this world. It is a carrying-on of the law of the Incarnation.

HILAIRE BELLOC

SONNET

Almighty God, whose justice like a sun
Shall coruscate along the floors of Heaven,
Raising what's low, perfecting what's undone,
Breaking the proud and making odd things even.
The poor of Jesus Christ along the street
In your rain sodden, in your snows unshod,
They have nor hearth, nor sword, nor human meat,
Nor even the bread of men: Almighty God.

The poor of Jesus Christ whom no man hears
Have waited on your vengeance much too long.
Wipe out not tears but blood: our eyes bleed tears.
Come smite our damned sophistries so strong
That thy rude hammer battering this rude wrong
Ring down the abyss of twice ten thousand years.

G. K. CHESTERTON

❧❧❧❧❧❧❧❧❧❧❧❧❧❧❧❧❧❧❧❧❧❧❧❧

THE RIDDLES OF THE GOSPEL

We have all heard people say a hundred times over, for they never seem to tire of saying it, that the Jesus of the New Testament is indeed a most merciful and humane lover of humanity, but that the Church has hidden this human character in repellent dogmas and stiffened it with ecclesiastical terrors till it has taken on an inhuman character. This, I venture to repeat, is very nearly the reverse of the truth. The truth is that it is the image of Christ in the churches that is almost entirely mild and merciful. It is the image of Christ in the Gospels that is a good many other things as well. The figure in the Gospels does indeed utter in words of almost heartbreaking beauty his pity for our broken hearts. But they are very far from being the only sort of words that he utters. Nevertheless they are almost the only kind of words that the Church in its popular imagery ever represents him as uttering. That popular imagery is inspired by a perfectly sound popular instinct. The mass of the poor are broken, and the mass of the people are poor, and for the mass of mankind the main thing is to carry the conviction of the incredible compassion of God. But nobody with his eyes open can doubt that it is chiefly this idea of compassion that the popular machinery of the Church does seek to carry. The popular imagery carries a great deal to excess the sentiment of "Gentle Jesus, meek and mild." It is the first thing that the outsider feels and criticises in a Pietà or a shrine of the Sacred Heart. As I say, while the art may be insufficient, I am not sure that the instinct is unsound. In any case, there is something appalling, something that makes the blood run cold, in the idea of having a statue of Christ in wrath. There is something insupportable even to the imagination in the idea of turning the corner of a street or coming out into the spaces of a marketplace, to meet the petrifying petrifaction of *that* figure as it turned upon a generation of vipers, or that face as it looked at the face of a hypocrite. The Church can reasonably be justified therefore if she turns the most merciful face or aspect towards men; but it is certainly the most merciful aspect that she does turn.

And the point is here that it is very much more specially and exclusively merciful than any impression that could be formed by a man merely reading the New Testament for the first time. A man simply taking the words of the story as they stand would form quite another impression; an impression full of mystery and possibly of inconsistency; but certainly not merely an impression of mildness. It would be intensely interesting; but part of the interest would consist in its leaving a good deal to be guessed at or explained. It is full of sudden gestures evidently significant except that we hardly know what they signify; of enigmatic silences; of ironical replies. The outbreaks of wrath, like storms above our atmosphere, do not seem to break out exactly where we should expect them, but to follow some higher weather-chart of their own. The Peter whom popular Church teaching presents is very rightly the Peter to whom Christ said in forgiveness "Feed my lambs." He is not the Peter upon whom Christ turned as if he were the devil, crying in that obscure wrath, "Get thee behind me, Satan." Christ lamented with nothing but love and pity over Jerusalem which was to murder him. We do not know what strange spiritual atmosphere or spiritual insight led him to sink Bethsaida lower in the pit than Sodom. I am putting aside for the moment all questions of doctrinal inferences or expositions, orthodox or otherwise; I am simply imagining the effect on a man's mind if he did really do what these critics are always talking about doing; if he did really read the New Testament without reference to orthodoxy and even without reference to doctrine. He would find a number of things which fit in far less with the current unorthodoxy than they do with the current orthodoxy. He would find, for instance, that if there are any descriptions that deserve to be called realistic, they are precisely the descriptions of the supernatural. If there is one aspect of the New Testament Jesus in which he may be said to present himself eminently as a practical person, it is in the aspect of an exorcist. There is nothing meek and mild, there is nothing even in the ordinary sense mystical, about the tone of the voice that says, "Hold thy peace and come out of him." It is much more like the tone of a very business-like lion-tamer or a strong-minded doctor dealing with a homicidal maniac. But this is only a side issue for the sake of illustration; I am not now raising these controversies; but considering the case of the imaginary man from the moon to whom the New Testament is new.

Now the first thing to note is that if we take it merely as a human story, it is in some ways a very strange story. I do not refer here to its tremendous and tragic culmination or to any implications involving triumph in that tragedy. I do not refer to what is commonly called the miraculous element; for on that point philosophies vary and modern philosophies very decidedly waver. Indeed the educated Englishman of today may be said to have passed from an old fashion, in which he would not believe in any miracles unless they were ancient, and adopted a new fashion in which he will not believe in any miracles unless they are modern. He used to hold that miraculous cures stopped with the first Christians and is now inclined to suspect that they began with the first Christian Scientists. But I refer here rather specially to unmiraculous and even to unnoticed and rather inconspicuous parts of the story. There are a great many things about it which nobody would have invented, for they are things which nobody has ever made any particular use of; things which if they were remarked at all have remained rather as puzzles. For instance there is that long stretch of silence in the life of Christ up to the age of thirty. It is of all silences the most immense and imaginatively impressive. But it is not the sort of thing that anybody is particularly likely to invent in order to prove something; and nobody so far as I know has ever tried to prove anything in particular from it. It is impressive, but it is only impressive as a fact; there is nothing particularly popular or obvious about it as a fable. The ordinary trend of hero-worship and myth-making is much more likely to say the precise opposite. It is much more likely to say (as I believe some of the gospels rejected by the Church do say) that Jesus displayed a divine precocity and began his mission at a miraculously early age. And there is indeed something strange in the thought that he who of all humanity needed least preparation seems to have had most. Whether it was some mode of the divine humility, or some truth of which we see the shadow in the longer domestic tutelage of the higher creatures of the earth, I do not propose to speculate; I mention it simply as an example of the sort of thing that does in any case give rise to speculations, quite apart from recognised religious speculations. Now the whole story is full of these things. It is not by any means, as baldly presented in print, a story that is easy to get to the bottom of. It is anything but what these people talk of as a simple Gospel. Relatively speaking, it is the Gospel that has the mysticism and the Church that has the rationalism. As I should put it, of course, it is the Gospel that is the riddle and the Church that is the answer. But whatever is the answer, the Gospel as it stands is almost a book of riddles.

First, a man reading the Gospel sayings would not find platitudes. If he had read, even in the most respectful spirit, the majority of ancient philosophers and of modern moralists, he would appreciate the unique importance of saying that he did not find platitudes. It is more than can be said even of Plato. It is much more than can be said of Epictetus or Seneca or Marcus Aurelius or Appollonius of Tyana. And it is immeasurably more than can be said of most of the agnostic moralists and the preachers of the ethical societies; with their songs of service and their religion of brotherhood. The morality of most moralists, ancient and modern, has been one solid and polished cataract of platitudes flowing for ever and ever. That would certainly not be the impression of the imaginary independent outsider studying the New Testament. He would be conscious of nothing so commonplace and in a sense of nothing so continuous as that stream. He would find a number of strange claims that might sound like the claim to be the brother of the sun and moon; a number of very startling pieces of advice; a number of stunning rebukes; a number of strangely beautiful stories. He would see some very gigantesque figures of speech about the impossibility of threading a needle with a camel or the possibility of throwing a mountain into the sea. He would see a number of very daring simplifications of the difficulties of life; like the advice to shine upon everybody indifferently as does the sunshine or not to worry about the future any more than the birds. He would find on the other hand some passages of almost impenetrable darkness, so far as he is concerned, such as the moral of the parable of the Unjust Steward. Some of these things might strike him as fables and some as truths; but none as truisms. For instance, he would not find the ordinary platitudes in favour of peace. He would find several paradoxes in favour of peace. He would find several ideals of non-resistance, which taken as they stand would be rather too pacific for any pacifist. He would be told in one passage to treat a robber not with passive resistance, but rather with positive and enthusiastic encouragement, if the terms be taken literally; heaping up gifts upon the man who had stolen goods. But he would not find a word of all that obvious rhetoric against war which has filled countless books and odes and orations; not a word about the wickedness of war, the wastefulness of war, the appalling scale of the slaughter in war and all the rest of the familiar frenzy; indeed not a word about war at all. There is nothing that throws any particular light on Christ's attitude towards organised warfare, except that he seems to have been rather fond of Roman soldiers. Indeed it is another perplexity, speaking from the same external and human standpoint, that he seems to have got on much better with Romans than he did with Jews. But the question here is a certain tone to be appreciated by merely reading a certain text; and we might give any number of instances of it.

The statement that the meek shall inherit the earth is very far from being a meek statement. I mean it is not meek in the ordinary sense of mild and moderate and inoffensive. To justify it, it would be necessary to go very deep into history and anticipate things undreamed of then and by many unrealised even now; such as the way in which the mystical monks reclaimed the lands which the practical kings had lost. If it was a truth at all, it was because it was a prophecy. But certainly it was not a truth in the sense of a truism. The blessing upon the meek would seem to be a very violent statement; in the sense of doing violence to reason and probability. And with this we come to another important stage in the speculation. As a prophecy it really was fulfilled; but it was only fulfilled long afterwards. The monasteries were the most practical and prosperous estates and experiments in reconstruction after the barbaric deluge; the meek really did inherit the earth. But nobody could have known anything of the sort at the time—unless indeed there was one who knew. Something of the same thing may be said about the incident of Martha and Mary; which has been interpreted in retrospect and from the inside by mystics of the Christian contemplative life. But it was not at all an obvious view of it; and most moralists, ancient and modern, could be trusted to make a rush for the obvious. What torrents of effortless eloquence would have flowed from them to swell any slight superiority on the part of Martha; what splendid sermons about the Joy of Service and the Gospel of Work and the World Left Better than We Found It, and generally all the ten thousand platitudes in favour of taking trouble—by people who need take no trouble to utter them. If in Mary the mystic and child of love Christ was guarding the seed of something more subtle, who was likely to understand it at the time? Nobody else could have seen Clare and Catherine and Teresa shining above the little roof at Bethany. It is so in another way with that magnificent menace about bringing into the world a sword to sunder and divide. Nobody could have guessed then either how it could be fulfilled or how it could be justified. Indeed some freethinkers are still so simple as to fall into the trap and be shocked at a phrase so deliberately defiant. They actually complain of the paradox for not being a platitude.

But the point here is that if we *could* read the Gospel reports as things as new as newspaper reports, they would puzzle us and perhaps terrify us *much* more than the same things as developed by historical Christianity. For instance: Christ after a clear allusion to the eunuchs of eastern courts said there would be eunuchs of the kingdom of heaven. If this does not mean the voluntary enthusiasm of virginity, it could only be made to mean something much more unnatural or uncouth. It is the historical religion that humanises it for us by experience of Franciscans or of Sisters of Mercy. The mere statement standing by itself might very well suggest a rather dehumanised atmosphere; the sinister and inhuman silence of the Asiatic harem and divan. This is but one instance out of scores; but the moral is that the Christ of the Gospel might actually seem more strange and terrible than the Christ of the Church.

I am dwelling on the dark or dazzling or defiant or mysterious side of the Gospel words, not because they had not obviously a more obvious and popular side, but because this is the answer to a common criticism on a vital point. The freethinker frequently says that Jesus of Nazareth was a man of his time, even if he was in advance of his time; and that we cannot accept his ethics as final for humanity. The freethinker then goes on to criticise his ethics, saying plausibly enough that men cannot turn the other cheek, or that they must take thought for the morrow, or that the self-denial is too ascetic or the monogamy too severe. But the Zealots and the Legionaries did not turn the other cheek, any more than we do, if so much. The Jewish traders and Roman tax-gatherers took thought for the morrow as much as we do, if not more. We cannot pretend to be abandoning the morality of the past for one more suited to the present. It is certainly not the morality of another age, but it might be of another world.

In short, we can say that these ideals are impossible in themselves. Exactly what we cannot say is that they are impossible for us. They are rather notably marked by a mysticism which, if it be a sort of madness, would always have struck the same sort of people as mad. Take, for instance, the case of marriage and the relations of the sexes. It might very well have been true that a Galilean teacher taught things natural to a Galilean environment; but it is not. It might rationally be expected that a man in the time of Tiberius would have advanced a view conditioned by the time of Tiberius; but he did not. What he advanced was something quite different; something very difficult; but something no more difficult now than it was then. When, for instance, Muhammad made his polygamous compromise we may reasonably say that it was conditioned by a polygamous society. When he allowed a man four wives he was really doing something suited to the circumstances, which might have been less suited to other circumstances. Nobody will pretend that the four wives were like the four winds, something seemingly a part of the order of nature; nobody will say that the figure four was written for ever in stars upon the sky. But neither will anyone say that the figure four is an inconceivable ideal; that it is beyond the power of man to count up to four; or to count the number of his wives and see whether it amounts to four. It is a practical compromise carrying with it the character of a particular society. If Muhammad had been born in Acton in the nineteenth century, we may well doubt whether he would instantly have filled that suburb with harems of four wives apiece. As he was born in Arabia in the sixth century, he did in his conjugal arrangements suggest the conditions of Arabia in the sixth century. But Christ in his view of marriage does not in the least suggest the conditions of

Palestine in the first century. He does not suggest anything at all, except the sacramental view of marriage as developed long afterwards by the Catholic Church. It was quite as difficult for people then as it is for people now. It was much more puzzling for people then than to people now. Jews and Romans and Greeks did not believe, and did not even understand enough to disbelieve, the mystical idea that the man and the woman become one sacramental substance. We may think it an impossible or incredible ideal; but we cannot think it any more incredible or impossible than they would have thought it. In other words, whatever else is true, it is not true that the controversy has been altered by time. Whatever else is true, it is emphatically not true that the ideas of Jesus of Nazareth were suitable to his time, but are no longer suitable to our time. Exactly how suitable they were to his time is perhaps suggested in the end of his story....

The truth is that when critics have spoken of the local limitations of the Galilean, it has always been a case of the local limitations of the critics. He did undoubtedly believe in certain things that one particular modern sect of materialists do not believe. But they were not things particularly peculiar to his time. Doubtless it would be nearer still to the truth to say merely that a certain solemn social importance, in the minority disbelieving them, is peculiar to our time. He believed, for instance, in evil spirits or in the psychic healing of bodily ills; but not because he was a Galilean born under Augustus.

It is absurd to say that a man believed things because he was a Galilean under Augustus when he might have believed the same things if he had been an Egyptian under Tuten-kamen or an Indian under Genghis Khan. It is enough to say that the materialists have to prove the impossibility of miracles against the testimony of all mankind, not against the prejudices of provincials in North Palestine under the first Roman Emperors. What they have to prove, for the present argument, is the presence in the Gospels of those particular prejudices of those particular provincials. And, humanly speaking, it is astonishing how little they can produce even to make a beginning of it.

So it is in this case of the sacrament of marriage. We may not believe in sacraments, as we may not believe in spirits, but it is quite clear that Christ believed in this sacrament in his own way and not in any current or contemporary way. He certainly did not get his argument against divorce from the Mosaic law or the Roman law or the habits of the Palestinian people. It would appear to his critics then exactly what it appears to his critics now; an arbitrary and transcendental dogma coming from nowhere save in the sense that it comes from him. I am not at all concerned here to defend that dogma; the point here is that it is just as easy to defend it now as it was to defend it then. It is an ideal altogether outside time; difficult at any period; impossible at no period. In other words, if anyone says it is what might be expected of a man walking about in that place at that period, we can quite fairly answer that it is much *more* like what might be the mysterious utterance of a being beyond man, if he walked alive among men.

I maintain, therefore, that a man reading the New Testament frankly and freshly would *not* get the impression of what is now often meant by a human Christ. The merely human Christ is a made-up figure, a piece of artificial selection, like the merely evolutionary man. Moreover there have been too many of these human Christs found in the same story, just as there have been too many keys to mythology found in the same stories. Three or four separate schools of rationalism have worked over the ground and produced three or four equally rational explanations of his life. The first rational explanation of his life was that he never lived. And this in turn gave an opportunity for three or four different explanations; as that he was a sun-myth or a corn-myth or any other kind of myth that is also a monomania. Then the idea that he was a divine being who did not exist gave place to the idea that he was a human being who did exist. In my youth it was the fashion to say that he was merely an ethical teacher in the manner of the Essenes, who apparently had nothing very much to say that Hillel or a hundred other Jews might not have said; as that it is a kindly thing to be kind and an assistance to purification to be pure. Then somebody said he was a madman with a Messianic delusion. Then others said he was indeed an original teacher because he cared about nothing but Socialism; or (as others said) about nothing but Pacifism. Then a more grimly scientific character appeared who said that Jesus would never have been heard of at all except for his prophecies of the end of the world. He was important merely as a Millenarian; and created a provincial scare by announcing the exact date of the crack of doom. Among other variants on the same theme was the theory that he was a spiritual healer and nothing else; a view implied by Christian Science, which has really to expound a Christianity without the Crucifixion in order to explain the curing of Peter's wife's mother or the daughter of a centurion. There is another theory that concentrates entirely on the business of diabolism and what it would call the contemporary superstition about demoniacs; as if Christ, like a young deacon taking his first orders, had got as far as exorcism and never got any further. Now each of these explanations in itself seems to me singularly inadequate; but taken together they do suggest something of the very mystery which they miss. There must surely have been something not only mysterious but many-sided about Christ if so many smaller Christs can be carved out of him. If the Christian Scientist is satisfied with him as a spiritual healer and the Christian Socialist is satisfied with him as a social reformer, so satisfied that they do not even expect him to be anything else, it looks as if he really covered rather more ground than they could be expected to expect. And it does seem to me that there might be more than they fancy in these other mysterious attributes of casting out devils or prophesying doom.

We should have a worse shock if we really imagined the nature of Christ named for the first time. What should we feel at the first whisper of a certain suggestion about a certain man? Certainly it is not for us to blame anyone who should find that first wild whisper merely impious and insane. On the contrary, stumbling on that rock of scandal is the first step. Stark staring incredulity is a far more loyal tribute to that truth than a modernist metaphysic that would make it out merely a matter of degree. It were better to rend our robes with a great cry against blasphemy, like Caiaphas in the judgment, or to lay hold of the man as a maniac possessed of devils like the kinsmen and the crowd, rather than to stand stupidly debating line shades of pantheism in the presence of so catastrophic a claim. There is more of the wisdom that is one with surprise in any simple person, full of the sensitiveness of simplicity, who should expect the grass to wither and the birds to drop dead out of the air, when a strolling carpenter's apprentice said calmly and almost carelessly, like one looking over his shoulder: "Before Abraham was, I am."

WILLIAM LANGLAND

❧ ❧

POVERTY AS THE BEST LIFE

I move this matter most of all for poor folk,
For in their likeness our Lord often has been discovered.
Witness in the Pascal Week, when he walked to Emmaus.
Cleophas did not recognize Christ before them
Through his poor apparel and pilgrim garments,
Till he blessed and broke the bread that they were eating.
They were aware by his works that he was Jesus,
But they could not tell him by his talk and clothing.

All this was in example to us sinful people
That we should all be lowly and loving in our speaking,
And not apparel us over proudly, for we are pilgrims
together.
God has many times been met among needy people
In the apparel of a poor man and in a pilgrim's likeness,
But never a soul has seen him in the sect of rich folk.

Saint John and other Saints were seen in poor clothing,
And were pilgrims praying for men's almsdeeds.
Jesus alighted upon a Jew's daughter of gentle lineage,
Yet a pure and poor maid, and wedded to a poor man.

Martha moved a complaint against Mary Magdalene
And said such words to our Saviour himself:
Domine, non est tibi curae quod soror mea reliquit me solam ministrare.
God answered hastily that he followed either,
Both Mary's way and Martha's way, as Matthew bears witness,
But God put poverty first and praised it more highly.
Maria optimam partem elegit, quae non, etc.
All the wise men that ever were, by aught that I can witness,
Praise poverty as the best life, if patience follow it,
As by far the more blessed and better than riches.
Although it is sour to suffer, sweet comes after,
There is a rough rind around the walnut,
But after that bitter bark has been shelled away
There is a kernel of comfort which conduces health—
So after poverty or penance patiently suffered;
For that makes men mindful of God, and more truly willing
To weep and to pray well, whence mercy arises.

And thus Christ is the kernel and comfort of the spirit.
The poor man sleeps more soundly and safely than others.
He dreads death, darkness and robbers
Less than he who is rich, as reason witnesses:
Pauper ego ludo, dum tu dives meditaris.

LÉONCE DE GRANDMAISON, S.J.

SON OF MAN

The form under which the testimony of Jesus is offered must remain enigmatic, and even incomprehensible, to anyone who does not recall the restless, wholly material and national, even chimerical character of the hopes of Israel at that time. Apart from this setting, how can we explain the safeguards, the qualifications, the reticence, or (to use the word adopted by the ancient Fathers in this connection) the economy, employed by Jesus in the affirmation of his mission and the revelation of his dignity?

The whole Jewish world was then expecting a Messiah, and this expectation had, on the showing of pagan historians, overflowed through all the East and beyond. How simple it would have been to say: "I am he!"

But in place of that categorical assertion, what do we see? The Master imposes silence on those possessed with spirits who proclaim him "the Holy One of God" (Mark 1:25), the

"Son of God" (Mark 3:11–12), "Jesus, Son of the Most High God" (Mark 5:7), etc. We hear him forbid his disciples to make him known as the Messiah (Mark 8:30; 9:8); he avoids the eagerness of the crowds (Mark 1:36–38; 8:10; John 6:14–16); and he deliberately extinguishes the fame of his miracles (Mark 1:41–44; 5:43; 7:32–36). Finally we see him, while proclaiming the advent of the Kingdom of God, at times eluding, as a distasteful subject, direct questions concerning his own part in the establishment of this Kingdom. At this point the reader of the Gospels is tempted to share the feeling expressed by a group of impatient hearers: "How long wilt thou hold our souls in suspense? If thou art the Christ, tell us so openly!" (John 10:24).

But Jesus had at least two reasons for not so acting, the first unconnected with the second. Let us recall the characteristics by which we have already described the Herodians on the one hand and the Zealots on the other; let us realise what was the situation in Palestine. In those divided, stormy surroundings, in which the watchword of one party was "Above all, no connection with Rome!", and in which the feverish expectation of the others anticipated the coming of a warrior-king who would drive the Gentiles from the Holy Land, a resounding Messianic claim on his part would have aroused their fears and galvanized their hopes. Thence would spring troubles and violent repressions, which Jesus did not wish to break out until the hour fixed by Providence: nor was it the object of his mission to quell them by force of miracles. Even as it was, in spite of the "economy" he used, the Master had more than once to flee the indiscreet enthusiasm of the people. Did they not talk of taking him and proclaiming him king? . . .

That is why Jesus, faithful to the idea of the Kingdom which he was to describe in the parables of the leaven and of the mustard-seed, adopted a rigid economy in the statement of his personal message. Following the footsteps of the ancient prophets and of John, he began by stirring up in men of good will, who were already moved by the Baptist's preaching, that uneasiness, that fruitful disquiet, that compunction, that hunger and that thirst for justice which, according to the Scriptures, was to mark the dawn of the Kingdom of God. For pictures of prosperity, of revenge, and of external glory, he substituted more humble, more intimate, more personal views, an indispensable preparation for the understanding of and inclination to accept the Gospel. Meanwhile, from the very beginning of his preaching, the Master performed those works of kindness, of deliverance, and of power, foretold by the great seers of the past. In view of these works and of the attitude of John the Baptist, to which we have drawn attention, the words of Andrew and Simon Peter could not but mount spontaneously to the lips of those who with uprightness and simplicity awaited the Hope of Israel: "We have found the Messiah!" (John 1:41). Thus were fulfilled the descriptions in Isaiah:

> *The spirit of the Lord is upon me.*
> *Wherefore he hath anointed me to preach the gospel to the poor:*
> *He hath sent me to preach deliverance to the captives and sight to the blind,*
> *to set at liberty them that are bruised,*
> *to preach the jubilee year of the Lord.*
> (Luke 4:18–19; Is. 61:1ff.)

Had not this jubilee year of the Lord arrived? The poor were evangelized, the sick healed, devils expelled, spirits set at liberty by the fall of the literalist burdens of human origin which weighted the yoke of the Law. Jesus had only to let the facts speak: but while he guided the minds of his hearers towards the complete truth, he avoided premature declarations, repulsed the unworthy homage of impure spirits, and tried the growing faith of his apostles, which for some time yet was to waver between eclipse and sudden brilliance.

But the Master needed, in this progress towards the light, some name which should indicate him without compromising him, which should stimulate minds without misleading them, and whose Messianic character should be real but not provoking. Through the Gospels we know that he chose that of "Son of Man." It is, as a matter of fact, certain that the Saviour habitually, and, as far as we can judge, from the beginning of his ministry, used this title, or if you will (to avoid prejudging anything) this designation, when speaking of himself. Persevering efforts have been made in recent times to eliminate this unusual phrase from Jesus's vocabulary, or at least to restrict and postpone its use. But the facts are opposed. We need only recall the chief ones: this expression, which (with one exception, which confirms the rule) is always put in the Master's own mouth, abounds in all the Gospels, John as well as the Synoptists, and in every part of them. It then disappears from the New Testament, only appearing once in the *Acts*, when the dying Stephen sees "the heavens opened and the Son of Man sitting on the right hand of God," and in the Johannine Apocalypse, in two analogous visions. Then its character is so clearly Semitic that St. Paul is compelled to give it a hellenistic transcription; and all ancient Christian tradition substitutes clearer and more explicit designations, such as "Lord," "Son of God," and even "Son of David" and "Servant" or "Child of God." All this proclaims its authenticity as an archaic and obscure term, and one which, far from offering a temptation to introduce it into the texts, has to be explained or even replaced by other expressions.

This fact once placed beyond doubt, it remains for us to discover the meaning given by Jesus to the expression. "Son of Man" is the exact equivalent of "man," and its use is no doubt due to the strict laws of Hebrew parallelism. Three times it is found in the Scriptures with this meaning. In Ezekiel it recurs, employed in the vocative, over and over again with a shade of pity, accentuating "the contrast between the majesty of God who is speaking, the fragility of the instrument he uses, and the grandeur of the part which that instrument is called upon to play" (E. Tobac, *Les Prophètes d'Israël*).

When the expression reappears in the celebrated passages of Daniel it takes a vaguer sense, strictly that of a being having the figure of a man, at least a man in exterior aspect. The second of these passages brings on the scene the archangel Gabriel under human form, appearing and acting as a "son of man," that is to say as a man. There remains, then, the first, which, by reason of its greater importance, must be transcribed in its context.

In the first year of Baltassar, king of Babylon, the prophet dreams a dream which he puts briefly into writing. The great sea stretches in front of him, and from the four cardinal points, "the four winds" which stir up the ocean, four powerful Beasts rise up in the shape of a winged lion, a bear, a panther with four wings, and finally a horned monster which changed its appearance. Then thrones are set and God, the Eternal, the Ancient of Days, surrounded by an imposing array, takes his place. The Beasts are judged; the fourth is condemned and cast into the flames, the others, their power taken away, survive for a time. Now while Daniel "considered these visions of the night,

> Lo, one like a son of man came with the clouds of heaven. And he came even to the Ancient of Days; and they presented him before him. And he gave him

> power, and glory and a kingdom: and all peoples, tribes, and tongues shall serve him. His power is an everlasting power that shall not be taken away: and his kingdom that shall not be destroyed. (Dan. 8:13–14)

One of those standing by then explains to the prophet that the four Beasts represent four empires, and that to their rule should succeed the sovereignty of the Most High and of his saints, which shall never fail:

> The kingdom and the power, and the greatness of the kingdom under the whole heaven, may be given to the [people of the] saints of the Most High. Whose kingdom is an ever-lasting kingdom. (Dan. 7:27. The words within brackets are disputed.)

This vision outlines in a striking picture the ancient prophetic scheme of Messiahship. The principal figure in the picture, whose function is to represent the visible element by means of which the eternal sovereignty of Jahveh will be exercised, is presented to the seer "like a son of man." ...

Ezra Chapter Four, an apocalypse which reflects with rare breadth of view the feelings of the Israelites who were not converted to Christianity, after the ruin of Jerusalem in 70, shows us a human figure who gloriously accomplishes the work of the Messiah emerging from the sea and coming "with the clouds of heaven," with an appearance which indubitably identifies him with Daniel's "son of man." Later rabbinical tradition, which is meagre enough—and with good reason, for the text of Daniel had become common ground for Christian apologetics—is none the less clear in the same sense....

The name "Son of Man" was capable of a Messianic sense through its use in the prophecy of Daniel and in some interpretations of later literature, but in no way by its actual form. It was closely related to the phrase familiar in the prophets, especially from Ezekiel onwards: "Son of Man!"—that is, "Man born of woman! man whose life is a breath!" Thus it was of itself alone a sort of parable, an enigma, a *mashal* of a type of which Hebrew tradition offers many examples. It raised problems, even if it did not of itself solve any; for Jesus used it to arouse the attention of the hearers and not to satisfy their curiosity. While effectively uniting the person and the mission of Jesus with the highest Messianic prerogatives of the universal Lord and Judge, it also brought out in relief those characteristics of apparent weakness, of gracious brotherhood, of redemptive suffering, and, in a word, of humanity, which must in reality mark the Master's life.

KARL ADAM

GOD THE SON

I

It is evident that, since Jesus refers Daniel's prophecy of the Son of Man to himself, his consciousness transcends all bounds of human possibilities and his claims reach up to the clouds of heaven, to the right hand of God himself.

Indeed, they reach still farther. It is highly significant that Jesus's conception of himself as the Son of Man is by no means coincident with Daniel's prophecy, nor exhausted by it. So exalted, so profound, so rich is the reality which lives in him that it goes far beyond Daniel's picture and gives the old phrase *Son of Man* a deepened sense and a new import. When, that is to say, Jesus calls himself the Son of Man, he is by no means only looking, as in Daniel's prophecy, to the coming end of time and its glory. Not one half of his declarations about himself as the Son of Man have reference to the last judgment. For the most part they apply to his work of redemption in the present, quite in accordance with that fusion of the now and the hereafter, of time and eternity, which characterizes his preaching of the kingdom. When Jesus sets the present with its distress and sin in the clear, dazzling light of his last judgment and in the glory of the new kingdom, he knows himself to be the one who shall take away the distress and the sin, who shall redeem mankind for the new kingdom. As the Son of Man he is judge and Saviour in one. Hence his message even as it applies to the present is an evangel. "Blessed are the eyes which see the things that you see. For I say to you that many prophets and kings have desired to see the things that you see, and have not seen them" (Luke 10:23ff.). Since he, the Son of man, will hereafter be Lord and King of the Kingdom of God, he is already in the present the source of salvation. "Come to me, all you that labour, and are burdened, and I will refresh you" (Matt. 11:28). His eschatological task presupposes the Messianic. Or better still they postulate one another. Jesus is therefore fond of using the term Son of man when he is speaking of his redemptive work in the present. "The Son of man is come to seek and save that which was lost" (Luke 19:10). "The Son of man" is he who sows the good seed, the children of the new kingdom (Matt. 8:37). It is the right of the Son of man to liberate man's ethical and religious endeavour from all extraneous bonds, even a law so venerable as the law of the Sabbath. "The Son of man is Lord also of the Sabbath" (Mark 2:28). Further, the "Son of man" does even what God alone does, what to many of the Jewish scribes exceeded the power of the expected Messiah. He forgives sins. "That you may know that the Son of man hath power on earth to forgive sins [he saith to the sick of the palsy] I say to thee, Arise, take up thy bed, and go into thy house" (Mark 2:10–11). There is the same claim in his words to the sinful woman: "Thy sins are forgiven thee" (Luke 7:48). In the forgiving of sins the redeemership of the Son of man, which embraces the present world, reaches its apex, and his Messianic claims their strongest and most emphatic expression. Here Jesus attains not only to the right hand of God, but into his heart.

Since he is filled with the awareness that it is the will of the Father that the redeemership of the Son of man should be consummated in suffering and the Cross, that the Lord and king of the new kingdom must win for himself his own by shedding his own life's blood for them, he always calls himself the Son of man when he speaks about his Passion. Again and again, when predicting his Passion, he emphasizes the fact that "the Son of man must suffer." "The Son of man is not come to be ministered to but to minister and to give his life a ransom for many." To Jesus when saying this the picture Isaiah draws of the suffering servant of God and Daniel's prophecy of the Son of man blend into a single majestic vision. He who, with a self-confidence which has no parallel, sees himself at the end of time as judge of the world and Lord of the new kingdom, at the same time knows himself to be the one whom Isaiah foretold, who "hath borne the sins of many, and hath delivered his soul unto death" (Is. 53:11). In the one little phrase, Son of man, the homeliest thing which he could tell us of himself, in the term "man" are concealed the most tremendous contrasts in this consciousness he had of himself. Jesus knows himself to be exalted to the heavens, and he sees himself thrust down into the slime of the earth. He is come to rule; he is come to minister and to die. King of the kingdom is he, and yet man, indeed the slave of men.

We can now understand why Jesus took by preference the name Son of man that by its simple symbolism he might indicate what he intends to be for man: a man among men and yet their king, their judge, and their Saviour, a man from heaven. From this that other term by which his contemporaries expressed their belief in the king of the last age, namely the Messiah, that is the anointed, the Christ, took on a new meaning. Whereas the Jews, when in their eighteen-clause petition they prayed for the coming of the Christ, had in mind a restoration of the glories of the kingdom of David, Jesus saw this "Christ" only as the coming Son of man, as the saviour and judge of the world. It was in this sense that he took Peter's confession, "Thou art the Christ" (Mark 8:29; Luke 9:20), and because of its mysterious depth he attributed it to an inspiration from on high. "Flesh and blood hath not revealed it to thee, but my Father who is in heaven." It was in this sense that the first Christians took it over from Peter, and since that day there has been no sweeter name in heaven or on earth than "Jesus Christ." If the expression "Christ" had hitherto been cumbered by Jewish conceptions that the expected Messiah would be of earthly stock, it henceforth turned men's hearts to the Son of man, to the right hand of the Ancient of Days, to the Saviour of the present, the king and judge of the future.

This was the novel and revolutionary element in the claim of Jesus. It stands in the most direct contrast with what the Jews of his time, under the spur of their selfish nationalistic instincts, believed and hoped of their expected Messiah. In this too is to be sought the determining cause of the drama of Golgotha. Had Jesus claimed to be a Christ in the Jewish nationalistic sense of the term, he would not have been crucified, even though his claim had been disputed and disallowed. For according to the law applicable to the case, such a claim, even though baseless, was not blasphemy against God, and was therefore not a capital offence. It was only when Jesus in that grave hour not merely gave assent to the high-priest's question, "Art thou the Christ, the Son of the Living God?", but with that serene truth which was of his essence, added the further confession: "And you shall see the Son of man sitting on the right hand of the power of God, and coming with the clouds of Heaven"—it was only then that he gave unequivocal meaning and an unequivocal answer to the equivocal question of the high-priest, for this it was when regarded in connection with Jewish Messianic ideas. In his fetters he sees himself at the right hand of the power of God. Arraigned before an earthly judge, he knows himself to be on the judgment seat of God. Could there be a greater paradox, and a more atrocious offence? "Then the high-priest rent his garments, saying: He hath blasphemed, what further need have we of witnesses? Behold, now you have heard the blasphemy: What think you? But they answering said: He is guilty of death. Then they did spit in his face, and buffeted him."

Jesus died, Jesus had to die, because men were too petty, too narrow, too abject and too obtuse to comprehend his sublimity and his divinity. He died for these base men because he was the Son of man.

II

JESUS had sent out the seventy-two disciples to preach the gospel of the kingdom all over the country. They returned rejoicing with the news that evil spirits had been subject to them. And Jesus tells them that they should rather rejoice because their names were written in heaven. And "in that same hour he rejoiced in the Holy Ghost and said: I confess to thee, O Father, Lord of Heaven and earth, because thou hast hidden these things from the wise and prudent, and hast revealed them to the little ones. Yea, Father, for so it hath seemed good in thy sight. All things are delivered to me by my Father, and no one knoweth who the Son is but the Father; and who the Father is but the Son, and to whom the Son will reveal him. And turning to his disciples, he said: Blessed are the eyes which see the things that you see. For I say to you that many prophets and kings have desired to see the things that you see and have not seen them; and to hear the things that you hear, and have not heard them" (Luke 10:21ff.).

Jesus speaks here with a joy and a triumph past measure. The success of the seventy-two has proved to him that the Messianic seed is germinating, that belief in his mystery is awakening. Precisely in the fact that it is the "little ones" who believe in his name he sees a special sign of God's graciousness and compassion. And so, overcome by this love, he draws from the welling riches of his own nature, where this love has proved itself more creative than it has anywhere else. There are three glories with which the Father has invested him. "All things are delivered to me by my Father"—all things, all honour and greatness, all authority and power, mankind and all the angels. There is literally nothing which is held by the Father alone, nothing which does not belong also to Jesus. These words quoted by Luke, span infinities upon infinities. John explains and supplements them by other sayings of Jesus. "All things whatsoever the Father hath are mine" (John 16:15). "All my things are thine and thine mine" (John 17:10). "As the Father raiseth up the dead, and giveth life; so doth the Son also give life to whom he will. For neither doth the Father judge any man: but hath given all judgment to the son. That all may honour the Son, as they honour the Father" (John 5:2). "Thou hast given him power over all flesh, that he may give eternal life to all whom thou hast given him" (John 17:2).

And the second glory lies yet deeper. It is properly the source of the first. "No one knoweth who the Son is but the Father: and who the Father is but the Son." The Son has a reality to which, in its ultimate depths, no one has access save the Father alone. Conversely, the reality of the Father is revealed to the Son alone. Thus Father and Son stand in a wholly unique, exclusive communion, in which no one else has any part. And the uniqueness of their communion lies in the fact that they are Father and Son. Jesus here paraphrases his essential relation to the Father, making use of conceptions native to the Jewish people and to Hellenistic mysticism beyond their borders. According to them no perfect knowledge of God is possible to man. Only God can have such knowledge of himself. Man can only be known by God (cf. 1 Cor. 8:1ff.; Gal. 4:9). Quite otherwise, as Jesus here emphasizes, is his own relation to God. He and he alone has the same perfect knowledge of the Father as the Father has of him. And this knowledge is his because he and he alone is the Son. On the other hand, to men the reality of the Son is no less mysterious than that of the Father. So hidden and so inaccessible is it, that only One knows it, and this because he is the Father. If we strip this self-revelation of Jesus of its mystical covering, we find the kernel to be nothing but a clear, unequivocal attestation to the unique, essential relation of his person to the Father and of the Father to him. They alone know and possess and permeate one another down to the very depths of their being, because they alone stand in the relation of Father and Son to one another. What Jesus here reveals with sublime simplicity is congruent with those self-revelations of Jesus which St. John, the evangelist of the interior life, relates. "Do you not believe that I am in the Father and the Father in me?" (John 14:10). "Philip, he that seeth me, seeth the Father also" (John 14:9). "Neither me do you know, nor my Father: If you did know me, you would know my Father also" (John 8:19). "I know mine, and mine know me, and I know the Father" (John 10:14ff.). "Believe the works: that you may know and believe that the Father is in me and I in the Father" (John 10:38).

The third glory follows directly from this oneness of being which united the Father and the Son. It was given definitive expression in the same discourse in which Jesus bore witness to himself, when he said, "No one knoweth who the Father is but the Son, and to whom the Son will reveal him." In its deepest sense his teaching and that of the Christian religion is therefore summed up in the words, "through the Son to the Father." There is no other way to the Father but by the Son. Here, too, we catch in the synoptic account the voice of the Johannine Christ, a clear proof that St. John, the beloved disciple, has faithfully preserved and handed down to us the inmost thoughts of Jesus and the manner in which these were communicated to his disciples. To the question of Thomas, "Lord, how can we know the way?" Jesus answered, "I am the way, the truth, and the life. No man cometh to the Father but by me" (John 14:6). "Just Father, the world hath not known thee: but I have known thee: and these have known that thou hast sent me" (John 17:25).

With this the last veils have fallen from the mystery of Jesus.

Proceeding from his purely human, mental and moral nature, through his religious interior life, we have found our way to his supernatural mystery; to the Divinity of his nature, to the Son of man as the judge and Lord of the future and the Saviour of the present. We have seen that what was earthly in him was based upon the superterrestrial, and that only from this standpoint could his human life be made historically intelligible. His superterrestrial nature is in turn revealed to us as the mystery of his Sonship, as the one direct sharing in the nature of the Father, as a oneness with him. The enigma of his historical appearance has been resolved in his own words: "No one knows the Father but the Son"; "I and the Father are one."

At these words thoughts fail and our tongue stumbles. The conception they express is staggering. Once upon a time, within historical memory, there lived a man, thoroughly sound in mind and body, who was gifted with unusually lucid insight into the facts of existence, into the greatest as well as the least, and with extraordinarily keen understanding. He was a man who was more selfless and unself-seeking than anyone who has ever lived, and whose life was devoted to the service of the poor and the oppressed. And this healthy, clear-sighted, selfless man, from beginning to end of his life, knew himself to be the unique well-beloved Son of the Father, to be one who knew the Father as no other man could. More than this, there was once a man, within historical times, who, as a child of the Jewish people, knew of only one God of heaven and earth, of a unique Father in heaven, and stood in reverential awe before this heavenly Father: a man whose meat was to do the will of this Father, who from his earliest youth in good days and bad had sought and loved this will alone, whose whole life was one prayer; a man, further, whose whole being was so firmly united with this Divine will, that by its omnipotence he healed the sick and restored the dead to life; a man, finally, who was so intimately and exclusively dedicated to this will, that he never swerved from it, so that not even the slightest consciousness of sin ever oppressed him, so that never a cry for penance and forgiveness passed his lips, so that even in dying he begged pardon not for himself but for others. And this man from the intimacy of his union with God could say to afflicted mortals, "Thy sins are forgiven thee." And it was this holy man, utterly subject as he was to God throughout his whole life, absorbed as he was in God, awestruck as he stood before him, who asserted, as if it were the most natural and obvious thing in the world, that he was to be the judge of the world at the last day, that he was the suffering servant of God, nay more, that he was the only begotten Son of God and consubstantial with him, and could say of himself, "I and the Father are one."

Can we, may we, dare we give credence to this man? We are asked to believe in the Incarnation of God, that is to say, we are asked to accept the fact that God so humbled himself as to "empty" himself, to use St. Paul's words, of his Divine majesty (Phil. 2:7). Is it not our duty to conclude that a man was mistaken, though he were the holiest who ever lived, rather than to believe that God would humble himself so immeasurably? Is not a man here rising up against God? Is it not in the last resort unbelief, if we believe? Does not our vigilant, reverent sense of God's uniqueness and eternal majesty actually oblige us to refuse our assent and either, like Caiaphas, to rend our garments and to cry out "He hath blasphemed," or with his kindred to lament his madness? Must we not, with Chesterton, rather "expect the grass to wither and the birds to drop out of the air, when a strolling carpenter's apprentice says calmly and almost carelessly, like one looking over his shoulder: 'Before Abraham was, I am.' 'I and the Father are one'"?

We can only say that a man who at this point, when confronted with the paradox of God the all-perfect, all-holy, eternal, becoming a man, a carpenter, a Jew hauled before the court and crucified, shrinks away, can go no further, and breaks down, may be actually less remote from a living piety than one who coolly accepts all this and glibly repeats his Credo, or indeed than one who does homage to the noble humanity of Jesus yet has the temerity to pooh-pooh what Jesus said of himself as harmless rhetoric, the innocent exaggerations of a pious eccentric.

And yet, in this question of all questions, has man, for all his faith and his conception of God, really the last word? What does "conception of God" mean? Is it not itself man-created? Is not God greater than man's conception of God? Is not the wisdom of man folly in God's sight? How, if God willed to prove himself God and to reveal the infinity of his omnipotence and the measurelessness of his love by becoming for our sakes a creature, a man who allowed himself to be crucified? In the infinite possibilities of God all conceivable possibilities are included, even the possibility of a Bethlehem and a Golgotha. What if God demands of man precisely this belief in the unbelievable? Suppose it was in this unbelievable way, and in no other, that it was his will to break down our human pride, to shatter all our human standards of what is possible, and to bring our minds and being into subjection to himself, and to himself alone? We cannot ignore Jesus. He is a possibility of God's. And given the possibility that God appeared on earth, we can see clearly that the humanity of Jesus was the right, true, unique place for his theophany. For nowhere else do there appear all the attributes of God, his majesty and omnipotence, his compassion and grace, so purely and continuously as here. If God appeared on earth in the form of man, he can only have appeared in Jesus. Nor is this all. The Divine is shown in Jesus with such overflowing richness, such impressive force, such evident clarity that we should have to close our eyes to the evidence and impugn the possibility of a fact attested by history, if we would deny the Divinity of Jesus.

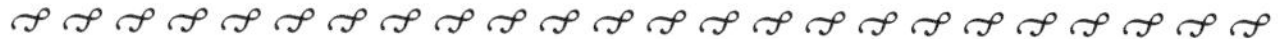

SOURCES OF THE SELECTIONS

F. J. Sheed's from *Theology and Sanity,* except the first section of the Prologue, which is from *A Map of Life.*

Hilaire Belloc's "Capharnaum and the Lake" from *Places;* "Sonnet" from *Sonnets and Verse.*

Caryll Houselander's "Philip Speaks" and "Matthew Speaks" from *The Flowering Tree.*

G. K. Chesterton's from *The Everlasting Man.*

C. C . Martindale's "True Son of Abraham" from *What Think Ye of Christ?;* "Life and the Food of Life" from *Creative Words of Christ.*

Leonce de Grandmaison's from *Jesus Christ.*

Walter Farrell's from *A Companion to the Summa.*

Karl Adam's "Perfect Man" and "God the Son" from *The Son of God.*

Eileen Duggan's from *Over the Bent World.*

Ronald Knox's "The Patience of Christ" from *A Retreat for Priests.*

Alfred Noyes' from *The Unknown God.*

P. R. Régamey's from *Poverty.*

Vincent McNabb's from *A Life of Our Lord.*

Poems not included in the above list will be found in *Poetry and Life: An Anthology.*

CLUNY MEDIA

Designed by Fiona Cecile Clarke, the Cluny Media *logo depicts a monk at work in the scriptorium, with a cat sitting at his feet.*

The monk represents our mission to emulate the invaluable contributions of the monks of Cluny in preserving the libraries of the West, our strivings to know and love the truth.

The cat at the monk's feet is Pangur Bán, from the eponymous Irish poem of the 9th century. The anonymous poet compares his scholarly pursuit of truth with the cat's happy hunting of mice. The depiction of Pangur Bán is an homage to the work of the monks of Irish monasteries and a sign of the joy we at Cluny take in our trade.

"Messe ocus Pangur Bán,
cechtar nathar fria saindan:
bíth a menmasam fri seilgg,
mu memna céin im saincheirdd."

Made in the USA
Columbia, SC
18 February 2023

12502737R00122